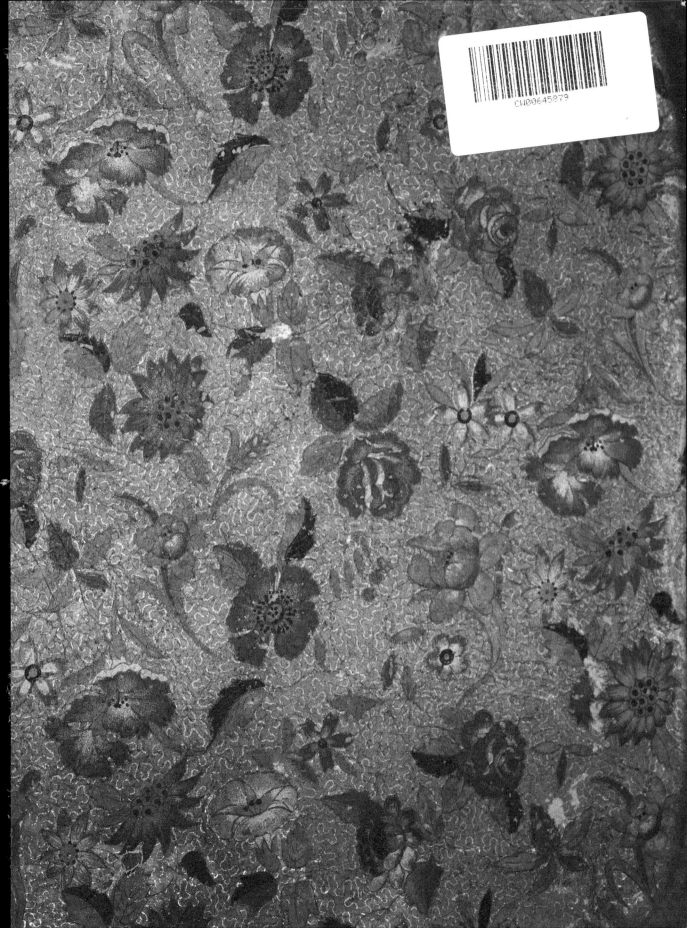

AVOCA
at Home

FOOD PHOTOGRAPHY - TREVOR HART

EDITORIAL PHOTOGRAPHY - DOREEN KILFEATHER

To our customers, for including Avoca in your
homes and family traditions over the years. All the
birthday celebrations, family dinners, anniversaries
and more that we've been lucky enough to play a
little part of – we're honoured – and so grateful.

This book is for you.

CONTENTS

INTRODUCTION

Over the years, the Avoca cookbooks have become dog-eared staples in Irish kitchens. For many of us Avoca food evokes fond memories, from the chicken and broccoli bake that was a Monday evening family favourite – to the decadent chocolate fudge cake a dear friend requested every year for their birthday. For lots of people, Avoca represents a feeling of *home*. It's the place you met your grandparents for tea and scones or where you went as a kid for your favourite traybake as a treat. It's the welcoming space for new mums to get together, for families who like to get out and about, stopping off for a late lunch on the way home. If you've moved away from Ireland, it's the place you head to when you're back home for a visit to meet friends and catch up over coffee.

Just as our cafés are much-loved, over the years our cookbooks have become the go-to source of recipes for comforting weeknight dishes, special occasion treats and everything in between. Now, with *Avoca at Home*, we are delighted to bring you a cookbook we're sure will become a new favourite, with a selection of our very best recipes. Exciting new dishes we know you'll love, classics with a contemporary twist and lots of tips on how to create the Avoca experience at home in your own way. From the soups and scones that put our name on the map to dishes inspired by far-flung adventures, we've set out to share simple, accessible and, most of all, *delicious* recipes with you and yours.

At Avoca we are proud to have been a part of Irish people's lives for centuries, right back to our beginnings as a rural weaving mill in Avoca Village, County Wicklow. In 1723, local sheep farmers banded together and established the mill where they would spin, dye and weave wool from their flocks to create beautiful blankets and clothing for their community. Today, we're honoured to still be a part of Irish homes – whether it's one of our throws draped over an armchair, a hand-prepared meal from our food markets becoming a weekly family treat or an Avoca cookbook taking pride of place in a kitchen.

At the heart of *Avoca at Home* is our unchanging food ethos – fresh, quality ingredients, Irish provenance and seasonality. These recipes have been created to spread the love of home-cooking and of sharing wholesome, indulgent, comforting food – to celebrate the joy of food and to relish the process. Though we've been stocking the pantries of Irish homes for over 30 years, we're always looking to the future. We delight at the thought of continuing our food journey in the years to come, offering the best of the best of Irish food, made with love and care, from our home to yours.

SAVVY SHOPPING &
STORE CUPBOARD STAPLES

Our food market shelves are stacked with the very best ingredients for all kinds of cooking, from spices, pastes and sauces to locally grown organic fruit and fresh vegetables. There will always be times when a last-minute dash to the shop is needed to get an unusual herb or a special spice. We've all been there when we're about to make an omelette only to realise that we forgot to pick up the eggs!

When it comes to trying a new recipe, our chefs recommend spending as much time shopping as you do cooking. Start with great ingredients – and, of course, you can pick up anything you need at our own food markets, which stock a wide range of artisanal and local products. We've built strong relationships not only with a host of local suppliers, but with many customers too. Familiar faces stop by each week, on first-name terms with our butchers, cheesemongers, wine experts and food market staff who are always on hand to share cooking tips, offer advice on cuts of meat or the best wine to pair with your favourite cheeses. If you're not near one of our food markets, you'll find fantastic outlets for fresh produce all over Ireland now – it's never been easier to source good-quality seasonal ingredients.

FAVOURITE ESSENTIALS THAT WE LOVE
TO HAVE IN OUR KITCHEN CUPBOARDS

COLD-PRESSED OILS – A selection of good-quality cold-pressed oils for cooking, dressing and drizzling. A great extra virgin olive oil goes without saying, but Irish rapeseed oil is also fantastic for cooking. For salad dressings or drizzling over grilled fish, nut oils are good, especially hazelnut and walnut oils.

PULSES & GRAINS – Every well-stocked store cupboard should have a selection of pulses and grains. From black beans and pinto beans for quick Mexican meals to split peas and lentils for soups and dahls, an assortment of tinned pulses and grains means you'll always be able to rustle something up at the last minute.

MIXED SEEDS – A selection of mixed seeds for toasting and sprinkling over salads, soups or porridge takes simple meals up a notch and adds a nice bit of crunch.

VINEGARS – A few types of vinegar always come in handy. For balsamic vinegar, we recommend finding one that's aged for that gorgeous, syrupy texture and deep flavour. Apple cider vinegar is also a staple to keep in the pantry. Both of these are useful for whipping up quick salad dressings.

DRIED CHILLIES– Dried chillies add heat to any stir-fries, curries or chilli con carne and they last for months.

IRISH SEA SALT – Go back to basics and choose a couple of excellent salts. Irish Atlantic Sea Salt is hard to beat! Season any dish with a generous sprinkle to take the flavour to the next level. It's simple to make your own flavoured salts at home too by adding fennel seeds, rosemary or dried chillies, perfect for seasoning roast meats and vegetables.

NUT BUTTERS – Nut butters are extremely versatile and can be used in a whole host of things, such as your morning smoothie, salad dressings and satays as well as countless baking recipes. They're also delicious smothered on sourdough toast for that 4 o'clock slump!

CHOPPING – A large wooden chopping board is both useful and beautiful. Once you've finished using it for your cooking prep, it makes a stunning sharing platter or serving board for bread, cheese or nibbles.

BREAKFAST & BRUNCH

Morning rituals are to be savoured. Whether
you're preparing a weekday bite to kickstart your
day or luxuriating over a slow Sunday breakfast
in bed, these recipes will help you to begin
every day as you mean to go on: enjoying every
bite. Our Avoca cafés are famous for decadent,
delicious brunches. Try your hand at some of our
favourites to recreate a taste of Avoca at home.

Lazy mornings
with *dippy eggs.*

Our Famous Avoca Scones

Makes 4 to 6

Scones might just be the first thing you think of when you think of Avoca. From the humble beginnings of our food markets, our freshly baked scones have always been a firm favourite. There was considerable debate among our bakers when it came to making our final scone selection for this book. The only thing you'll be divided on is how you pronounce the word 'scone'!

METHOD

Preheat the oven to 180°C. Line a baking tray with non-stick baking paper.

Put the flour, sugar, baking powder and salt in a large bowl and stir to combine, then add the butter and rub it into the dry ingredients until it looks like breadcrumbs.

Add the beaten eggs to the dry ingredients along with the milk, then knead gently to bring together into a soft dough. You may need to add a little more flour if the dough is too wet or a splash of milk if it's too dry.

Turn out the dough onto a lightly floured work surface. Shape into a circle and pat it down until it's 2.5cm thick, then cut into six small or four large scones. Place the scones on the lined tray, then brush with the beaten egg and sprinkle with the sugar.

Bake in the preheated oven for 20 minutes, until golden brown and risen. Allow to cool on a wire rack. Serve warm.

Continues ...

500g plain flour
50g caster sugar
1 heaped tsp baking powder
¼ tsp fine sea salt
110g butter, cubed, at room temperature
2 large eggs, beaten
200ml milk

For the topping:
1 egg, beaten
10g caster sugar

VARIATIONS

Berry & Cinnamon Scones

Add ½ teaspoon of ground cinnamon to the dry
ingredients, then add 100g of frozen mixed berries with
the beaten eggs and milk.

Pear & Almond Scones

Add 100g of diced tinned pears and ¼ teaspoon of vanilla
extract with the beaten eggs and milk. Brush with the
eggwash, sprinkle over the extra sugar and scatter some
flaked almonds on top.

Chocolate & Orange Scones

Simmer 2 whole Valencia oranges in a large saucepan of
boiling water for about 1 hour, until very soft. Drain and
allow to cool, then blitz in a blender or food processor until
smooth (you need 150g of pulp in total). Add 2 teaspoons
of cocoa powder to the dry ingredients. After rubbing in the
butter, add just one beaten egg, the orange pulp and 100g of
milk chocolate chips, then pour in 100ml of milk. Use the
tines of a fork to drizzle over some melted milk chocolate
and scatter with a little orange zest after they come out of
the oven if you like.

Date & Apple Scones

Makes 4 to 6

A more virtuous option, our date and apple scones are lower in sugar due to the natural sweetness of the dates. Prepare the dry mix ahead of time – up to a week in advance – then all you have to do is add the milk, yogurt and apple.

METHOD

Preheat the oven to 180°C. Line a baking tray with non-stick baking paper.

Put the apple in a small saucepan with the caster sugar and cook over a medium heat for 6 to 8 minutes, until the cubes have softened slightly but are still holding their shape. Remove the pan from the heat and allow to cool.

Put the flour, dates, oats, bran, brown sugar and baking powder in a large bowl and mix together. Add the butter and rub it into the dry ingredients until it looks like breadcrumbs.

Whisk the yogurt and milk together, then add to the dry ingredients along with the cooked apple and stir to combine. Knead gently to bring together into a soft dough. You may need to add a little more flour if the dough is too wet or a splash of milk if it's too dry.

Turn out the dough onto a lightly floured work surface. Shape and cut into six small or four medium scones.

Place the scones on the lined tray, then brush with a little milk and sprinkle over some brown sugar and oats.

Bake in the preheated oven for 20 minutes, until golden brown and risen. Allow to cool on a wire rack.

1 medium-sized eating apple, peeled, cored and cut into 1cm cubes
1 tbsp caster sugar
400g plain flour
200g dates, pitted and chopped
60g porridge oats, plus extra for the topping
60g wheat bran
60g light brown sugar, plus extra for the topping
1 tbsp baking powder
60g butter, diced
250ml Greek yogurt
150ml milk, plus extra for brushing

Bircher Muesli
with Cacao Nibs & Espresso

Serves 4 to 6

Combine your breakfast and your caffeine hit. Topped with creamy Greek yogurt and flaked almonds and Cacao Nibs for a bit of crunch, this tasty, nutritious breakfast is a win-win. For a little extra sweetness, add a spoonful of your favourite jam or conserve.

METHOD

Place the oats in a large bowl and grate in the apple, then stir in the almond milk, espresso, maple syrup and cinnamon. Cover the bowl with cling film and leave in the fridge overnight to let the oats absorb all the liquid and flavours.

To serve, divide the Bircher between six breakfast bowls or pots. Top each serving with a tablespoon of Greek yogurt, a sprinkle of cacao nibs and some toasted flaked almonds, then drizzle with maple syrup.

220g porridge oats
1 Granny Smith apple
550ml almond milk
45ml espresso
5 tbsp maple syrup
1 tsp ground cinnamon

For the topping:
6 tbsp Greek yogurt
2 tbsp cacao nibs
2 tbsp toasted flaked almonds
maple syrup

Why not try this handy storage tip?

SERVE & STORE

Recycle your jam jars and use them to serve your Bircher muesli, or pop the lid on and take it on the go.

Best Ever Granola

Makes 12 large portions

Our award-winning granola isn't called the 'best ever' for nothing! Packed with dried fruit, nuts, seeds and more, it's a delicious breakfast option topped with Greek yogurt, served with fruit or as a crunchy sprinkle over porridge. You can also add a handful to a smoothie.

METHOD

Preheat the oven to 140°C.

Line two baking trays with non-stick baking paper.

Mix the seeds and almonds together in a large bowl, then stir in the oats and mix to combine.

Put the honey, coconut milk, sunflower oil and orange oil in a small saucepan over a low to medium heat and warm gently to loosen. Pour onto the oats, mixing thoroughly so that all the dry ingredients are evenly coated. Divide between two baking trays and spread it out in an even layer.

Bake in the preheated oven for 1 hour, removing the trays from the oven and stirring the granola on the trays every 20 minutes.

Allow to cool a bit on the trays, then mix the granola with the dried apricots and cranberries until evenly combined and allow to cool completely.

Store in an airtight container. It can be kept for up to three months if stored correctly.

VARIATION

Super Berry Granola

Make exactly as per the recipe above but omit the dried apricots and stir in 50g of dried goji berries, 15g of freeze-dried raspberries and 15g of freeze-dried strawberries after the granola comes out of the oven and has cooled a bit.

50g pumpkin seeds
50g sunflower seeds
50g sesame seeds
50g flaxseeds
50g whole almonds
400g porridge oats
220g honey
200ml tinned coconut milk
40ml sunflower oil
a few drops of orange oil
200g dried apricots, diced
200g dried cranberries

Our Famous Fern House Pancakes

Serves 4 to 6

Slow down your Sunday morning with warm homemade pancakes and soft sheets for the most heavenly breakfast in bed. These buttermilk pancakes are a long-standing favourite in the Fern House Café at Avoca Kilmacanogue. Pancakes are such a treat and are made even more so with fresh blueberries, berry compote and a macadamia nut praline.

METHOD

Preheat the oven to 160°C. Line a small baking tray with non-stick baking paper and have it sitting on your countertop, ready to go for the praline.

Scatter the macadamia nuts on a baking tray and toast in the oven for 10 minutes, until light golden.

Meanwhile, put the sugar and water in a medium-sized saucepan over a medium heat. Allow it to cook without stirring until it begins to turn a medium-brown colour. This could take up to 10 minutes. It will continue to cook and reach a deeper brown, so don't let it go too dark. Turn off the heat and swirl the melted sugar gently around the pot – don't stir it or the caramel might clump up.

Once the caramel is ready, add the butter and allow it to melt, swirling to combine, then add the toasted macadamia nuts. Immediately pour it out onto the baking paper and spread it out with a spatula as best you can, then sprinkle with a pinch of flaky sea salt and let it cool. Caramel is molten hot, so do not be tempted to lick the spoon! Once the praline has cooled and hardened, break it into small pieces and set aside.

Continues ...

430g plain flour
85g icing sugar
4 tsp baking powder
4 eggs
550ml buttermilk
55g unsalted butter
a splash of sunflower oil
120g fresh blueberries

For the macadamia praline:
100g macadamia nuts
160g caster sugar
50ml water
½ tsp butter
a pinch of flaky sea salt

For the berry compote:
250g fresh or frozen strawberries
60g fresh or frozen raspberries
60g fresh or frozen blueberries
50g caster sugar

To serve:
Greek yogurt
maple syrup

METHOD CONTINUED

To make the berry compote, put all the berries and the sugar in a small saucepan and bring to the boil. Turn down the heat and simmer for about 5 minutes, crushing the berries with a wooden spoon. If using frozen berries, cover the pan and cook for 10 minutes to thaw the berries, then remove the cover and continue to simmer. The compote should be reduced and thick, more like a syrup than a jam, and it will thicken as it cools. Remove from the heat and set aside.

To make the pancakes, sieve the flour, icing sugar and baking powder together into a large bowl.

Whisk the eggs and buttermilk together, then fold this into the dry ingredients until you have a smooth batter but take care not to overmix or your pancakes will be tough.

Melt some of the butter and a splash of oil in a large non-stick frying pan over a medium heat. Working in batches so that you don't overcrowd the pan, add spoonfuls of the batter and cook 1 minute before sprinkling a few blueberries on top of each one, pushing them down gently into the batter. Cook for about 2 minutes more – when you see bubbles forming on top of the pancakes, flip them over and cook the other side for 2–3 minutes, until golden. Repeat with the rest of the butter and the batter.

To serve, stack up the pancakes on plates and spoon over some Greek yogurt and berry compote. Drizzle with maple syrup and top with the macadamia nut praline.

Huevos Rancheros

Serves 4

A classic Mexican dish, huevos rancheros is the perfect breakfast or brunch for those who like that extra kick.

METHOD

To make the pico de gallo, simply mix all the ingredients together, season with salt and pepper and set aside.

Heat 2 tablespoons of oil in a large frying pan over a medium heat. Add the onion, red pepper, serrano pepper and a pinch of salt and cook for about 5 minutes, until slightly softened. Add the tomatoes and season to taste, then cook for 10 to 12 minutes more, until the tomatoes have broken down into a sauce. Keep warm.

Meanwhile, to make the refried beans, heat the 2 tablespoons of rapeseed oil in a separate large frying pan over a medium heat. Add the garlic and cook for just 1 minute, until fragrant, then add the pinto beans, cumin and chilli powder. Cook for 6 to 8 minutes, until the beans are heated through, then mash with a potato masher directly in the pan. Stir in the lime juice and season with salt and pepper.

To finish, put a frying pan over a medium-high heat. Working with one or two corn tortillas a time, depending on how big your pan is, cook them for about 30 seconds on each side, just until they're soft and pliable, or according to the packet instructions. Transfer to a plate and cover with a cloth to keep warm.

In the same pan, cook the eggs to your liking – we think that sunny side up with crispy edges is best.

To assemble, load each tortilla with the refried beans, then top with an egg. Spoon over the warm tomato and pepper sauce, then add some pico de gallo on top or on the side. Lastly, scatter over the diced avocado and chopped fresh coriander.

2 tbsp rapeseed oil
1 medium onion, diced
1 red pepper, diced
1 serrano pepper, deseeded and diced
4 large vine-ripened tomatoes, chopped
fine sea salt and freshly ground
    black pepper

For the pico de gallo:
2 medium vine-ripened tomatoes,
    deseeded and finely diced
½ red onion, finely diced
1 jalapeño pepper, finely diced (or a little
    diced green pepper if you don't like
    too much heat)
2 tbsp chopped fresh coriander
juice of ½ lime

For the refried beans:
2 tbsp rapeseed oil
1 garlic clove, finely chopped
1 x 400g tin of pinto beans,
    drained and rinsed
1 tsp ground cumin
1 tsp chilli powder
juice of ½ lime

To serve:
8 corn or flour tortillas
4 to 8 medium eggs (depending
    on whether you want 1 or
    2 eggs per serving)
1 avocado, peeled, stoned and diced
2 tbsp chopped fresh coriander

Why not try a different spin on this?

SWITCH IT

Corn tortillas are best, but plain flour tortillas are delicious too.

Baked Eggs
with Ham & Cheese

Serves 4

How do you like your eggs in the morning? We like ours baked with ham and cheese! This is a great brunch dish to use up little leftover pieces of ham or corners of cheese. Be adventurous and try different combinations – chorizo and Manchego cheese works really well.

METHOD

Preheat the oven to 200°C. Grease the inside of four ramekins with butter.

Divide the chopped ham and cheese between the four ramekins, then top each one with a teaspoon of cream and season with a pinch of salt and pepper. Crack an egg into each ramekin.

Place the ramekins on a baking tray, then place on the middle rack of the preheated oven. Cook for 12 to 15 minutes, until the whites are set and the yolks are cooked to your liking.

Serve with a final crack of black pepper and oversized toast soldiers on the side for dipping.

2 tsp butter, for greasing
80g cooked ham, chopped
80g smoked Gubbeen cheese, chopped
4 tsp cream
4 medium eggs
fine sea salt and freshly ground black pepper

To serve:
oversized toast soldiers

Croque Monsieur

Makes 4

Bring a little *je ne sais quoi* to your breakfast table – grab some sourdough or your favourite crusty bread, some Gruyère cheese and thick slices of roast ham, softened butter, for spreading, *et voilà!*

METHOD

Preheat the oven to 170°C. Line a baking tray with non-stick baking paper. Butter all eight slices of bread on one side, setting four slices to one side for now. Set aside 40g of the grated Gruyère as well.

Put four slices of bread butter side down, then scatter over a layer of cheese, then a slice of a ham, then another layer of cheese and another slice of ham. Set aside.

To make the béchamel, gently heat the milk in a small saucepan, taking care not to let it boil.

Melt the butter in a separate medium-sized saucepan over a medium heat. Add the flour and cook for about 2 minutes, stirring, until it has become a golden-brown paste and the raw flour taste has cooked out. Gradually pour in the hot milk, whisking after each addition. Once all the milk has been added, keep stirring until it's thickened and smooth. Stir in the mustard and season with the salt and pepper.

Add a heaped tablespoon of the béchamel to each open sandwich, then top with the reserved four slices of sourdough, butter side up.

Heat a large non-stick frying pan over a medium-high heat. Working in batches, add a sandwich to the hot pan, butter side down. Cook each sandwich for about 90 seconds just on this side.

Transfer each sandwich to the lined baking tray, cooked side down. Add a heaped tablespoon of the remaining béchamel to the top of each sandwich, spread it evenly over the surface, and top with the reserved Gruyère. Cook in the preheated oven for 10 to 12 minutes, until golden brown.

Serve with a lightly dressed crisp green salad and Avoca Tomato Chutney on the side.

8 slices of sourdough or crusty
  bread
160g grated Gruyère cheese
16 slices of cooked ham

For the béchamel:
280ml milk
2 tbsp butter
2 tbsp plain flour
1 tsp Dijon mustard
fine sea salt and freshly
  ground pepper

To serve:
lightly dressed green salad
Avoca Tomato Chutney

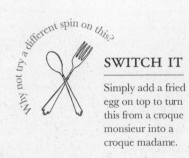

Why not try a different spin on this?

SWITCH IT

Simply add a fried egg on top to turn this from a croque monsieur into a croque madame.

Smoked Salmon & Poached Eggs

with Punchy Caper Salsa

Serves 4

Deliciously simple, the only 'cooking' involved in this recipe is poaching the eggs and toasting the sourdough to go on the side. If you want to poach your eggs ahead of time, transfer the cooked eggs to a large bowl of iced water to stop them cooking any further. When you need them, simply place them in a saucepan of hot water for 40 to 50 seconds to warm them through again.

METHOD

To make the salsa, simply mix together the tomatoes, red onion and capers with a little brine from the jar of capers and season with salt and pepper.

Brush both sides of the sourdough bread with the oil and toast in a hot chargrill pan over a high heat for about 90 seconds on each side, then divide the sliced smoked salmon between the four slices of toasted sourdough.

Crack the eggs into separate ramekins or cups. Fill a wide saucepan two-thirds full of water and bring to the boil, then add the vinegar. As soon as it comes to the boil, turn the heat down to a very low simmer and carefully slide four of the eggs into the water. Cook for 3 to 4 minutes, until the whites are set but the yolks are still runny. Use a slotted spoon to transfer the poached eggs to a plate lined with kitchen paper to drain while you cook the other four eggs.

To serve, add two poached eggs on top of each slice of smoked salmon-draped toast and finish with a spoonful of the salsa.

4 large slices of sourdough
4 tbsp rapeseed oil
200g smoked salmon
$\frac{1}{4}$ tsp pepper
8 large eggs
1 tbsp white wine vinegar

For the punchy caper salsa:
3 vine-ripened tomatoes, diced
$\frac{1}{2}$ medium red onion, finely
  diced
2 tbsp capers
fine sea salt and freshly ground
  black pepper

Chorizo & Baby Potato Hash

with Preserved Lemon Yogurt & Dukkha

Serves 4

A hearty and flavoursome breakfast hash, the preserved lemon yogurt cuts through the rich chorizo while the dukkha provides a hit of North African spice. Try serving this dish family-style for sharing.

METHOD

To make the dukkha, toast the nuts in a hot dry frying pan over a high heat. Do not add any oil. Toast for a few minutes, shaking the pan to keep the nuts moving and taking care not to let them burn. Tip the nuts out into a bowl, then add all the seeds to the hot pan and toast for 1–2 minutes, again keeping the pan moving to toast them evenly. Add them to the bowl with the nuts and allow to cool.

Transfer the cooled toasted nuts and seeds to a pestle and mortar or a food processor. Pound or pulse the mix just until it resembles large breadcrumbs, but not too much as dukkha should not be a powder.

To make the preserved lemon yogurt, simply mix the finely chopped lemon and yogurt and allow it to sit in the fridge, covered with cling film, until needed.

Steam the baby potatoes until just cooked but still firm – this should take 20 to 25 minutes. Alternatively, you can cook them for 10 to 15 minutes in a pan of boiling salted water. Drain and allow to cool, then cut into 5cm chunks.

Meanwhile, set a large frying pan over a medium heat without any oil. When the pan is nice and hot, add the chorizo and cook for 5 minutes. When the chorizo has

Continues ...

1kg baby potatoes
200g dry-cured Spanish chorizo, diced
2 medium red onions, roughly chopped
1 to 2 tbsp rapeseed oil
2 garlic cloves, finely chopped
4 eggs, cooked to your liking
fine sea salt and freshly ground black pepper

For the dukkha:
100g blanched hazelnuts
100g blanched almonds
100g shelled pistachios
40g sesame seeds
4 tsp fennel seeds
4 tsp cumin seeds
4 tsp coriander seeds

For the preserved lemon yogurt:
30g preserved lemon, pips removed and finely chopped
4 heaped tbsp Greek yogurt

METHOD CONTINUED

released its oil and crisped up a bit, add the onions and a pinch of salt and cook for about 5 minutes more, until softened. Add 1 or 2 tablespoons of rapeseed oil if the pan looks too dry for cooking the onions. Add the garlic and cook for 1 minute, just until fragrant. Remove the chorizo, onions and garlic from the pan and set aside, but do not remove the oil.

Add the cubed potatoes, increase the heat to medium-high and cook for 10 minutes, stirring every minute or so. When the potatoes have turned golden and crisp, add the chorizo, onions and garlic back to the pan, season to taste with salt and pepper and stir to combine, then reduce the heat to low to keep everything warm.

Cook the eggs to your liking. We serve them sunny side up with this dish in our restaurants, but poached eggs work well too (see page 40 for instructions on how to poach eggs).

Divide the potato and chorizo hash between four wide, shallow bowls and add an egg to each. Dollop a tablespoon of the preserved lemon yogurt on top and sprinkle over the nutty dukkha.

VARIATION

Poached Egg & Halloumi Hash

For a vegetarian version, swap the chorizo for 450g of halloumi cut into eight slices, brushed with 30g of harissa paste and charred on a smoking hot griddle pan over a high heat for 2 minutes on each side. Dice a red pepper and cook it with the red onions and ½ teaspoon of smoked paprika.

We think you'll love this...

EXTRA EXTRA

The leftover dukka is delicious for sprinkling on fish, steaks, salads and avocado toast. Just store it in an airtight container.

SOUPS & BREAD

Nothing summons people to the kitchen like a
bubbling pot of soup on the stove, particularly
as the evenings get darker and chillier. There's
a hearty, warming bowl of soup for every mood
here as well as a couple of our most-loved bread
recipes, perfect for dunking. Here's hoping there's
enough left for second helpings.

Cold hands wrapped around *warm* bowls.

White Onion & Parmesan Soup

Serves 4

This warming soup is one of our café favourites and perfect for those cooler autumn days.

METHOD

Melt the butter in a large heavy-based pot over a medium-low heat. Add the onions and garlic and cook gently for about 10 minutes, until the onions are translucent but not coloured.

Add the potatoes, stock, salt and white pepper. Simmer for 20 to 25 minutes, until the potatoes are cooked through and tender. Remove the pot from the heat, then stir in the Parmesan cheese and cream.

Using a hand-held blender, purée the soup until it's silky smooth. Check the seasoning and adjust to your taste.

Ladle the soup into warmed bowls and drizzle with a little white truffle oil. Serve with buttered slices of Avoca's famous brown bread on the side

80g butter
2 medium onions, peeled and chopped
1 garlic clove, peeled and finely chopped
4 large potatoes, peeled and cut into large dice
1 litre vegetable stock
1 tsp fine sea salt
½ tsp freshly ground white pepper
150g grated Parmesan cheese
350ml cream
good-quality white truffle oil, to garnish

To serve:
Avoca's famous brown bread
(page 66)

Avoca Chicken Broth

with Tubetti

Serves 4

A hug in a bowl, this chicken broth is packed with goodness and is good for the soul. A deliciously simple, humble lunch served with our famous Avoca brown bread slathered with butter, it's perfect for feeding the whole family.

METHOD

Start by making your stock. Place the whole chicken, vegetables, herbs and peppercorns in a large pot and cover with the cold water. Bring to the boil, then reduce the heat and simmer gently for 1 hour, taking care to remove all sediment or froth that comes to the top. Strain over a large bowl to keep all the stock, but discard the vegetables. Allow the chicken to cool before removing the meat from the bones. Shred the meat and set it aside to add back into the soup later.

Heat the olive oil in a large heavy-based saucepan over a low heat. Add the onion, carrots, celery, leek, bay leaf and thyme and cook gently for about 10 minutes, until the vegetables have softened. Add the turmeric and cook for another 2 minutes, stirring continuously so that the spice doesn't burn.

Meanwhile, cook the pasta in a separate pot of boiling salted water for 5 minutes, then drain and add to the pot with your soup base.

Pour in all your stock and bring it up to a simmer. Cook for about 15 minutes more, until the pasta is al dente. Add the shredded chicken and cook until it's piping hot.

Taste and adjust the seasoning as necessary and finish with the chopped fresh parsley just before serving with buttered slices of Avoca's famous brown bread on the side.

For the stock:
1 medium free-range chicken
1 large onion, peeled and
    cut into 6
2 celery stalks
2 large carrots
a couple of fresh parsley stalks
1 sprig of fresh thyme
8 black peppercorns
4 litres cold water

For the soup:
2 tbsp olive oil
1 medium onion, peeled and diced
2 large carrots, peeled and diced
2 celery stalks, diced
½ small leek, thinly sliced
1 bay leaf
2 tbsp fresh thyme leaves
¼ tsp ground turmeric
100g tubetti or macaroni pasta
3 tbsp chopped fresh flat-leaf
    parsley
fine sea salt and freshly ground
    black pepper

To serve:
Avoca's famous brown bread
    (page 66)

Spiced Chickpea Soup

Serves 8 to 10

A hearty soup that you can largely rustle up from the store cupboard. Roasting the tomatoes, aubergine, onion and garlic gives this soup a deliciously rich flavour and a hint of sweetness.

METHOD

Preheat the oven to 200°C.

Put the tomatoes, aubergine, onion and garlic on a baking tray, toss with 3 tablespoons of the oil and season with salt and pepper. Roast in the preheated oven for about 20 minutes, until softened.

Meanwhile, heat the remaining 3 tablespoons of oil in a large saucepan over a low heat. Add the carrot, celery, leek and red chilli and cook for about 5 minutes, until softened. Add the fresh herbs, ground cumin and coriander and the mustard seeds and cook for a further 5 minutes.

Add the tomato purée and cook for 1 or 2 minutes before pouring in the wine and vinegar. Let them bubble up to deglaze the pan, then stir in the chickpeas and stock along with the roasted vegetables. Bring to the boil, then reduce the heat and simmer for about 15 minutes. Use a hand-held blender to blitz until smooth, then taste and adjust the seasoning.

To serve, divide the soup between warmed bowls and top each portion with a tablespoon of crème fraîche and some chopped fresh coriander.

5 ripe plum tomatoes, peeled and
   cut into quarters
1 aubergine, cut into large pieces
1 onion, roughly chopped
4 garlic cloves, sliced
6 tbsp rapeseed oil
1 carrot, peeled and diced
2 celery stalks, sliced
1 leek, sliced
1 fresh red chilli, deseeded and
   finely chopped
1 sprig of fresh thyme
1 sprig of fresh rosemary
1 tsp ground cumin
1 tsp ground coriander
1 tsp mustard seeds
2 tbsp tomato purée
250ml white wine
1 tbsp rice wine vinegar
1 x 400g tin of chickpeas, drained
   and rinsed
1.5 litres vegetable stock
4 tbsp crème fraîche
2 tsp chopped fresh coriander
fine sea salt and freshly ground
   black pepper

One of our foodie favourites...

TASTE TIP

Try sprinkling some dukkha (page 43) over this soup as an additional garnish.

Tomato, Coconut & Harissa Soup

Serves 4

The smoky heat of the harissa is balanced by the cooling coconut milk, resulting in a light but creamy soup with a kick.

METHOD

Heat the rapeseed oil in a large saucepan over a medium heat. Add the onion, carrot, red pepper and a pinch of salt. Cover with a lid and cook for 5 minutes, until the vegetables have started to soften. Add the garlic, preserved lemon, harissa, sugar, cumin and chilli flakes and cook for 1 or 2 minutes more, just until fragrant.

Stir in the passata and water. Bring to the boil, then reduce to a simmer and cook for 5 minutes. Finally, stir in the coconut milk and continue to cook for another 2 to 3 minutes, until heated through.

Remove the pan from the heat and use a hand-held blender to blitz the soup until smooth.

To serve, divide the soup between four warmed bowls and drizzle a little extra virgin olive oil on top of each one.

4 tsp rapeseed oil
1 onion, roughly chopped
1 carrot, peeled and roughly chopped
1 red pepper, roughly chopped
3 garlic cloves, chopped
2 tsp finely chopped preserved lemon
2 tsp harissa paste
1 tsp caster sugar
1 tsp ground cumin
¼ tsp chilli flakes
1 x 700g jar of tomato passata
400ml water
1 x 400ml tin of light coconut milk
extra virgin olive oil, for drizzling
fine sea salt and freshly ground black pepper

Irish Minestrone
with Wild Nettle Pesto

Serves 6

The Irish twist on this classic Italian recipe is the nettle pesto. Just don't forget to bring thick gloves when you're foraging for this native Irish wildflower to avoid any nasty nettle stings. Of course, regular basil pesto works wonderfully too.

METHOD

First make the pesto. Use thick gloves to pick the nettles, then wash them thoroughly (a salad spinner would work well here).

Bring a saucepan of salted water to the boil, then add the nettles and blanch for 2 or 3 minutes. This will get rid of the formic acid and remove their sting. Drain in a colander, then squeeze out all the water (remember, they should be safe to handle now that the sting has been cooked out of them).

Put the blanched nettles in a food processor with the parsley, garlic, Parmesan and pine nuts. With the motor running, slowly pour in the oil. You may need to scrape down the sides of the food processor a few times with a spatula. You want the pesto to be quite thick. Season to taste with salt and pepper.

To make the minestrone, melt the butter and oil together in a large saucepan over a medium-high heat. Add the bacon and fry for 3 or 4 minutes, then use a slotted spoon to transfer it to a plate lined with kitchen paper to absorb any excess fat.

Lower the heat to medium, then add the onion, carrots, celery and leek. Cook for 10 minutes, until softened,

Continues ...

2 tbsp butter
2 tbsp rapeseed oil
6 bacon rashers (fat trimmed and discarded), chopped
1 medium onion, diced
3 small carrots, peeled and diced
2 celery stalks, diced
½ large leek, diced
2 garlic cloves, finely chopped
1 tbsp tomato purée
2 medium potatoes, diced
1.2 litres low-sodium vegetable stock
2 bay leaves
2 sprigs of fresh thyme
250ml tomato passata
80g macaroni pasta
60g of kale or cavolo nero, leaves stripped from the inner ribs and chopped
6 fresh basil leaves, torn

For the wild nettle pesto:
100g wild nettles
100g fresh flat-leaf parsley
1 garlic clove, chopped
1 tbsp grated Parmesan cheese, plus extra for serving
1 tbsp pine nuts, toasted
200ml rapeseed oil
fine sea salt and freshly ground black pepper

METHOD CONTINUED

then add the garlic and tomato purée and cook for 1 or 2 minutes more.

Add the bacon back in along with the potatoes, stock, bay leaves and thyme. Bring to the boil, then reduce the heat and cook for 15 minutes, until the potatoes are nearly cooked.

Stir in the passata, macaroni and kale (though if you're planning on cooking this ahead of time, cook the pasta separately and add it to the soup when you are reheating it). Cook for a further 10 to 15 minutes, until the pasta is cooked. Season to taste with salt and pepper, then stir in the basil.

To serve, divide the minestrone between warmed bowls, top with a generous spoonful of the wild nettle pesto and scatter over some extra grated Parmesan.

Why not try this handy storage tip?

SERVE & STORE

Leftover pesto can be stored in a sealed jar for up to a week.

Salmon Chowder

Serves 6

This salmon chowder is our take on the traditional brotchán roy with the addition of porridge oats. We know it might sound unusual, but trust us when we say it's delicious!

METHOD

Melt the butter in a large heavy-based saucepan over a medium heat. Add the onion and a pinch of salt and cook for about 10 minutes, until softened and translucent.

Add the leek, potato, oats, mace or nutmeg and some salt and white pepper and cook for 3 minutes, just to give the vegetables a bit of colour. Add the stock, raise the heat to medium-high and simmer for 10 minutes, until the potatoes are soft. Stir occasionally so the potatoes don't catch on the bottom of the pan.

Add the salmon and cream and simmer for 5 minutes, just until the salmon is cooked. Stir in the chopped parsley.

To serve, ladle into warmed bowls with slices of Avoca's famous brown bread on the side.

60g butter
1 onion, roughly chopped
1 large leek, roughly chopped
500g potatoes, cut into large bite-sized pieces
30g porridge oats
a pinch of ground mace or nutmeg
1 litre chicken or vegetable stock
500g salmon fillet, skinned and diced
150ml cream
2 tbsp chopped fresh flat-leaf parsley
fine sea salt and ground white pepper

To serve:
Avoca's famous brown bread (page 66)

One of our foodie favourites...

TASTE TIP

Add some prawns and mussels for a proper seafood treat.

Kale, Quinoa & White Bean Soup

Serves 4

You might think that kale and quinoa are healthy and virtuous, but we're firm believers that they can be absolutely delicious too. This soup will warm your bones and fill you up.

METHOD

Cook the quinoa in a pan of boiling water for 10 to 12 minutes, until fully cooked. Drain and rinse under cold running water, then set aside.

Meanwhile, heat the oil in a large saucepan over a medium heat. Add the onion, carrots and celery and cook for 10 to 15 minutes, until softened and translucent. Add the garlic, thyme and chilli flakes and cook for 1 or 2 minutes more, just until fragrant.

Stir in the tomato passata, cannellini beans and stock. Bring to the boil, then reduce the heat and simmer for 15 minutes to let all the ingredients come together. Add the cooked quinoa and the kale and cook for another 5 minutes, until the kale is wilted but still a bright, vibrant green.

Adjust the seasoning to taste with salt and pepper, then remove the pan from the heat and stir in the chopped parsley.

To serve, ladle into warmed bowls and garnish with a drizzle of extra virgin olive oil and Parmesan cheese shavings.

30g quinoa (or pearl quinoa if you can source it)
2 tbsp rapeseed oil
1 small onion, chopped
1 carrot, peeled and chopped
1 celery stalk, chopped
4 garlic cloves, finely chopped
1 tsp finely chopped fresh thyme
¼ tsp chilli flakes
1 x 500g carton of tomato passata
1 x 400 tin of cannellini beans, drained and rinsed
500ml vegetable or chicken stock
40g kale, leaves stripped from the inner ribs and chopped
2 tbsp finely chopped fresh flat-leaf parsley
fine sea salt and freshly ground black pepper

To garnish:
extra virgin olive oil
Parmesan cheese shavings

Waste not want not...

USE IT UP

Feel free to add any extra vegetables that need to be used up – they'll only make it more delicious.

Avoca's Famous Brown Bread

Makes 1 loaf

We simply couldn't share our best soups without including a recipe for our famous brown bread. One of the very first Avoca recipes, it's now over 30 years old and is still a firm favourite. For dipping, mopping and dunking, our brown bread is best sliced thick and slathered in Irish butter.

METHOD

Preheat the oven to 200°C. Grease a 2lb loaf tin well with oil or use a paper liner or a sheet of non-stick baking paper.

Mix all the dry ingredients together in a large bowl. Add the treacle and stir in most of the milk to create a moist mixture. You may not need to use all the milk.

Scrape into the greased or lined loaf tin and bake in the preheated oven for 20 minutes, until risen. Reduce the heat to 170°C and bake for a further 40 minutes.

Remove from the oven, run a knife around the tin and ease the bread out. If it sounds hollow when tapped on the bottom, it's done. If not, return it to the oven for 5 to 10 minutes more.

Allow to cool on a wire rack before cutting into slices to serve. This keeps well for a few days and makes the most delicious toast in the morning.

VARIATION

Multiseed Bread

Add a handful of seeds of your choosing to make a multiseed version. We like to use linseeds as well as pumpkin, sesame, sunflower and poppy seeds.

oil, for greasing
300g coarse wholemeal flour
200g plain flour
3 tbsp bran
2 tbsp wheat germ
2 heaped tsp baking powder
1 tsp fine sea salt
1 dessertspoon treacle
600ml milk

Focaccia

Serves 6

The beauty of focaccia is that you can be adventurous and make it your own – try adding olives, sun-dried tomatoes or even smoked garlic. Ideal for sharing and tearing, family style.

METHOD

Put the flour in the bowl of a stand mixer fitted with a dough hook. Add the yeast to one side of the flour and the fine salt on the other side, then mix everything together. (We separate the salt and the yeast, as salt can hinder the yeast's ability to activate.)

Make a well in the middle of the flour. Add 2 tablespoons of the extra virgin olive oil and 350ml of the warm water, mixing until you have a slightly sticky dough. Add the remaining 50ml of the water if needed to bring the dough together. Mix on a medium speed for 6 to 8 minutes, until you have a soft, smooth dough. (Alternatively, you can knead it by hand on a lightly floured countertop for 10 minutes.)

Lightly grease a large bowl. Put the dough into the bowl, cover with a clean tea towel and leave to prove in a warm place for 1 hour, until doubled in size. An airing cupboard often works well.

Grease a shallow rectangular tin (25cm x 35cm). Dust your countertop with a little flour, then knock back the dough and tip it out onto the countertop, stretching it to fill the tin. Transfer to the tin, cover with the tea towel and leave to prove again for 45 minutes, until risen.

Preheat the oven to 200°C.

Press your fingers into the dough to make dimples, leaving about 2.5cm between indentations. Brush the top with olive oil and sprinkle over the flaky sea salt. Push sprigs of rosemary into the dimples in the dough.

Bake in the preheated oven for 20 minutes, until golden. When the bread comes out of the oven, drizzle over another 2 tablespoons of olive oil. Cut into squares and serve with your favourite dishes or use for a gourmet sandwich.

500g strong white flour, plus extra for dusting
1 x 7g sachet of fast-action dried yeast
1 tsp fine sea salt
4 tbsp extra virgin olive oil, plus extra for greasing and brushing
400ml warm water (ideally at 40°C)
1 tbsp flaky sea salt
1 small bunch of fresh rosemary, cut into small sprigs

Flatbread

Makes 6

These are so simple to make and so versatile. Flatbreads are the perfect addition to the baba ghanoush, courgette fritters, falafel and tzatziki on the mezze board on pages 237–239, but they can also be used for gyros, souvlaki, flatbread pizzas … the list is endless.

METHOD

Heat the milk and butter together in a small saucepan over a medium heat just until the butter has melted.

Put the flour and salt in a large bowl and mix together, then pour in the warm milk and butter. Mix to bring together into a rough dough.

Dust your countertop with a little flour, then tip out the dough and knead for 3 to 4 minutes, until smooth. Wrap in cling film and allow to rest at room temperature for 30 minutes.

Divide the dough into six balls (about 70g each) and dust the countertop with flour again as well as a rolling pin. Roll each of the balls into an oval-shaped flatbread 5mm thick.

Heat the rapeseed oil in a large non-stick frying pan over medium heat. Working in batches, add one or two flatbreads to the pan at a time and cook for 1½ to 2 minutes on each side. Large bubbles might puff up on the bread as it cooks – simply press the air out of them with a spatula.

Once cooked, keep them wrapped in a clean tea towel. This will steam them slightly, making them soft and more pliable.

Brush the flatbreads with a little extra virgin olive oil and serve warm.

120ml milk
50g butter, melted
270g plain flour, plus extra for dusting
½ tsp fine sea salt
6 tbsp rapeseed oil
1 tbsp extra virgin olive oil, for brushing

SALADS & QUICHE

An iconic Avoca lunchtime duo, salads and
freshly baked quiche are an established staple in
our cafés and food markets. Familiar faces stop by
each week for a slice of quiche paired with their
favourite salads, so this combo is a must for a true
taste of Avoca at home.

Platefuls of
colour & *flavour.*

GROW YOUR OWN

We're always striving to get closer to the origins of food and where it comes from – literally. We grow a lot of our own ingredients at our vast kitchen garden at Avoca Dunboyne and in our grow beds at Avoca Kilmacanogue. We're passionate about good food, and that means using great ingredients grown in season. There's nothing quite like tucking into freshly dug new potatoes with lashings of butter, salt and pepper.

You don't need a huge garden or professional set-up to grow your own, though. There are so many ways to incorporate growing more of your own herbs and vegetables at home. Whether you have a vast outdoor space, a small balcony or even a sunny windowsill, you can grow something delicious – and we believe that any ingredient grown at home with a little love and care tastes a whole lot better.

SOME GROWING TIPS

from our gardeners, Des and Dermot

Sow what you like to eat. It might sound obvious but it's easy to get carried away, so stick to what you love to eat and cook.

If you want to get growing in a small space, greens are a wonderful option. Mizuna, rocket and red and green mustards are a great place to start – rocket can be ready to put on your plate in as little as 26 days. Of course, there's always an abundant return on herbs too. Rosemary, thyme and parsley are all easy to grow on small balconies or windowsills.

Let's talk about basil, or more specifically, watering it! Basil is gloriously simple to grow at home, but make sure you pop it on a sunny windowsill as it prefers to be behind glass. But above all, don't overwater it. Basil is a Mediterranean herb, so it thrives when it can dry out between watering. Don't worry if it wilts – it will perk back up again after watering, even after two weeks. It also grows well in empty old tomato tins, thanks to the iron.

One of our favourite ingredients at Avoca has got to be garlic and it's surprisingly simple to grow your own. Spanish varieties tend to be the easiest to care for. They can be planted in October or November and harvested towards the end of June.

Potatoes are another Avoca favourite! The secret with potatoes is to plant an early variety such as Duke of York or Sharpe's Express to avoid the blight that sets in every July. Traditionally, potatoes are planted on St Patrick's Day and harvested on the 29th of June.

Cavolo nero kale is also low maintenance. It's the perfect thing to grow in our Irish climate and tends not to be bothered by pests in the garden. Incredibly good for you, it's great for adding to juices and soups.

Rhubarb has made a comeback in recent times and is abundant when it's in season from early spring until late summer. It can be harvested in the second year after planting and for years thereafter and it freezes well too. Lifetime supply of rhubarb crumble, anyone?

Encourage kids to help you grow. Try starting with cress or mustard in recycled yogurt pots – kids love to watch it grow and you can use it to garnish sandwiches. If you have a larger garden, sunflowers and pumpkins are great fun. The little ones will love to watch the sunflowers grow taller than they are!

Baby Gem Wedge Salad
with Smoked Almond & Caper Gremolata

Serves 6

Crisp and fresh, this salad will almost transport you to Italy. To make it even simpler, you can prepare the yogurt dressing and the gremolata ahead of time.

METHOD

To make the herby yogurt dressing, put the mayonnaise, yogurt, mint, parsley, tarragon, lemon juice and garlic in a blender or food processor and blitz until smooth, then season to taste with salt and pepper.

To make the gremolata, put the smoked almonds, capers, parsley and lemon zest in a medium-sized bowl and toss to combine. Pour in the rapeseed oil and stir to bring everything together, then season with salt and pepper.

To serve, place one lettuce half on a plate. Spoon over the herby yogurt dressing, followed by the gremolata.

3 heads of baby gem lettuce,
  halved lengthways

For the herby yogurt dressing:
6 tbsp mayonnaise
3 tbsp Greek yogurt
3 tbsp chopped fresh mint
3 tbsp chopped fresh flat-leaf
  parsley
1 tbsp chopped fresh tarragon
juice of 1 lemon
1 garlic clove, chopped

*For the smoked almond
and caper gremolata:*
80g smoked almonds, roughly
  chopped
60g capers, roughly chopped
25g fresh flat-leaf parsley,
  chopped
zest of 1 lemon
3 tbsp rapeseed oil
fine sea salt and freshly ground
  black pepper

Shaved Beetroot & Blood Orange Salad

Serves 4 to 6

Simple to rustle up at a moment's notice, this beetroot salad packs a punch when it comes to vibrant colour and flavour. Avoid pink fingers by popping on a pair of gloves.

METHOD

To shave the beetroot, use the fine slicing blade on a food processor to get the best result. You may need to cut them in half to fit them down the chute. Alternatively, you can use a mandolin if you have one, but as always, use the finger guard and be extremely careful.

Toast all the seeds in a hot dry frying pan over a medium-high heat for 2 to 3 minutes, tossing the seeds constantly so they don't burn. Tip out onto a plate.

Put the yogurt in a large bowl. Add the shaved carrots and toss to coat, then place the carrots on a serving platter. Arrange the shaved beetroot and blood oranges over the top and sprinkle with the rocket and toasted seeds. Season with pepper but use the finely chopped salted capers as your seasoning.

To serve, garnish with the torn basil leaves and drizzle over a little more yogurt.

600g raw beetroot, peeled

4 tbsp sunflower seeds

4 tbsp pumpkin seeds

1 tbsp sesame seeds

2 tsp linseeds

100g natural yogurt, plus extra to garnish

2 medium carrots, peeled and shaved

4 blood oranges, peeled and sliced or segmented

80g rocket

a pinch of freshly ground black pepper

1 tsp finely chopped capers

6 fresh purple basil leaves, torn, plus extra to garnish

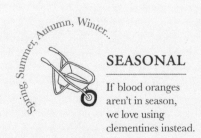

Spring, Summer, Autumn, Winter...

SEASONAL

If blood oranges aren't in season, we love using clementines instead.

Lentil, Kale & Green Apple Salad

Serves 8

Guaranteed to fill you up and give you an energy boost, this tasty salad is packed with goodness. The zesty, mustardy dressing provides zing, while the toasted hazelnuts and green apples give it a satisfying crunch.

METHOD

Preheat the oven to 160°C.

Scatter the hazelnuts over a small baking tray and toast in the preheated oven for 5 to 10 minutes, until golden. Tip out onto a plate and set aside to cool, then roughly chop.

Rinse the lentils under cold running water. Bring a saucepan of salted water to the boil, then add the lentils and reduce the heat. Simmer, uncovered, for 15 to 20 minutes, until tender. Once they are cooked, drain and cool them under cold running water.

Make the dressing by whisking together the lemon juice, oil, mustard and 2 tablespoons of the maple syrup. Taste and adjust the seasoning with salt and pepper and another tablespoon of maple syrup if you'd like it to be a little sweeter.

Place the apple slices in a large bowl and drizzle with the reserved lemon juice to prevent them from oxidising (turning brown). Add the toasted hazelnuts and cooked lentils to the apples along with the baby kale, raisins, parsley and tarragon.

Toss to combine, then pour over the dressing, season with salt and pepper and toss again to coat everything lightly with the dressing.

130g hazelnuts
400g beluga lentils
3 Granny Smith apples, halved, cored and thinly sliced
150g baby kale
120g golden raisins
4 tbsp chopped fresh flat-leaf parsley
2 tbsp chopped fresh tarragon

For the dressing:
juice of 2 lemons (reserve a little for the apples)
8 tbsp rapeseed oil
1 tbsp Dijon mustard
2 to 3 tbsp maple syrup
fine sea salt and freshly ground black pepper

When writing your shopping list...

SHOPPING

If you can't find beluga lentils, you could use the brown or Puy variety instead.

Butternut Squash & Bulghur Salad

with Fennel & Clementines

Serves 6

This salad covers all the bases when it comes to flavour. Vibrant and colourful, it's the perfect addition to any summer lunch or barbecue.

METHOD

Preheat the oven to 170°C.

Place the bulghur in a large heatproof bowl and pour over the just-boiled water, then add the oil and a good pinch of salt. Cover the bowl with cling film and let it sit for about 20 minutes, until all the water has been absorbed and the grain is tender.

Meanwhile, drizzle the butternut squash with a little oil and scatter over the chopped rosemary, then season with salt and pepper. Roast in the preheated oven for 12 to 14 minutes, until soft. Allow to cool completely.

To make the dressing, whisk together the oil, maple syrup, lemon zest and juice and the clementine zest, then season to taste with salt and pepper.

Put the cooked bulghur and roasted squash in a large mixing bowl along with the clementine slices, sliced fennel, pistachios (reserve some pistachios for garnish), chopped fresh herbs (hold some mint back for garnish too) and the nigella seeds. Pour over the dressing and toss to combine, then taste and adjust the seasoning.

Arrange on a large serving plate and garnish with the reserved pistachios and chopped mint.

400g bulghur
500ml just-boiled water
2 tbsp olive oil, plus extra
    for roasting
300g butternut squash,
    peeled and cut into 2cm cubes
1 tbsp chopped fresh rosemary
2 clementines, peeled and sliced
1 fennel bulb, very thinly
    sliced or shaved
100g pistachios, shelled and toasted
4 tbsp chopped fresh mint
4 tbsp chopped fresh flat-leaf
    parsley
2 tbsp chopped fresh dill
1 tbsp nigella seeds

For the dressing:
8 tbsp olive oil
2 tbsp maple syrup
2 lemons – zest of 1, juice of 2
zest of 2 clementines
fine sea salt and freshly ground
    black pepper

Roast Cauliflower & Chickpea Salad

with Spiced Yogurt Dressing

Serves 6

Roast cauliflower and spiced yogurt are a match made in heaven and it only gets better with a scattering of crunchy pistachios.

METHOD

Preheat the oven to 190°C.

Mix the garlic, curry powder, turmeric, fennel seeds and some salt and pepper with the oil and maple syrup to make a paste, then rub this all over the cauliflower florets. Place on a baking tray and roast in the preheated oven for about 10 minutes. Check the cauliflower with a knife – you want it to be tender but still have some bite to it, and keep in mind that it will continue to cook while it cools.

Reduce the oven temperature to 160°C. Scatter the pistachios over a small baking tray, then toast in the oven for 5 to 10 minutes.

Transfer the cooled cauliflower to a large bowl. Add the chickpeas along with most of the chopped fresh coriander and most of the toasted pistachios and toss to combine, then season lightly again. Add the lemon juice and a splash of olive oil to loosen the spices on the cauliflower, creating a dressing for your salad.

To make the yogurt dressing, toast the coriander and cumin seeds in a hot dry frying pan over a high heat for 2 or 3 minutes, until fragrant. Tip out onto a plate and allow to cool, then grind in a spice or coffee grinder. Add to the yogurt along with the lime juice and whisk to combine, then season to taste.

Transfer the salad to a serving bowl, then drizzle the spiced yogurt across the salad and garnish with the reserved pistachios and fresh coriander.

1 garlic clove, minced
1 tbsp curry powder
1 tbsp ground turmeric
1 tsp fennel seeds
4 tbsp olive oil, plus extra for drizzling
2 tbsp maple syrup
1 head of cauliflower, broken into bite-sized florets
120g shelled pistachios
2 x 400g tins of chickpeas, drained and rinsed
3 tbsp chopped fresh coriander
juice of ½ lemon
fine sea salt and freshly ground black pepper

For the yogurt dressing:
2 tbsp coriander seeds
2 tbsp cumin seeds
6 tbsp Greek yogurt
juice of 1 lime

One of our foodie favourites...

TASTE TIP

Sprinkle over some dukkha (page 43) as an additional garnish.

Just Peachy
with Shaved Fennel, Feta & Hazelnuts

Serves 6

Sweet, juicy, fresh, crumbly and nutty, this peachy salad is a treat in summertime. Try to find the most delicious, perfectly ripe peaches you can – they make all the difference.

METHOD

Preheat the oven to 180°C.

Scatter the hazelnuts on a baking tray and toast in the preheated oven for 8 to 10 minutes, until golden. Tip out onto a plate and set aside, then roughly chop.

Meanwhile, to make the dressing, whisk together the oil, orange juice, lemon juice, maple syrup and harissa paste, then taste and adjust the seasoning with salt and pepper. The dressing should have a perfect balance of heat from the harissa, acidity from the citrus and sweetness from the maple syrup.

Cut each peach in half and remove the stones, then slice each half into five segments. Put in a large bowl with the toasted hazelnuts, orange segments, fennel and nigella seeds and toss gently to combine.

Just before serving, add the baby salad leaves and fresh mint, and drizzle over the dressing and gently toss together. Transfer the salad to a serving dish and crumble the feta on top.

100g hazelnuts
3 ripe peaches (nectarines work well too)
2 oranges, segmented
1 fennel bulb, very thinly sliced
1 tbsp nigella seeds
150g mixed baby salad leaves
2 tbsp chopped fresh mint
60g feta cheese

For the dressing:
80ml olive oil
juice of 1 orange
juice of 1 lemon
1 tbsp maple syrup
1 heaped tbsp harissa paste
fine sea salt and freshly ground black pepper

We think you'll love this...

EXTRA EXTRA

Make a double batch of this dressing because you will love it!

Green Herb Goodness
Pasta Salad with Courgette & Pine Nuts

Serves 6

Packed with greens and goodness, this summery dish is perfect for serving alongside one of our delicious quiches for an al fresco lunch.

METHOD

Cook the pasta in boiling salted water for 8 to 10 minutes, until al dente, or according to the packet instructions. Drain and set aside to cool.

Toast the pine nuts in a hot dry frying pan over a medium heat for 2 to 3 minutes, then tip out onto a plate and allow to cool.

Blitz all the pesto ingredients together in a blender or food processor. It may seem like there's not enough liquid, but the moisture in the herbs themselves helps the pesto come together. This should take 3 to 4 minutes. Season to taste with salt and pepper.

Transfer the cooled pasta to a large serving bowl. Add the grated courgette and pesto, then toss to combine and coat. Top with the torn basil leaves and toasted pine nuts.

200g fusilli or spirali pasta
40g pine nuts, toasted
1 medium courgette, grated
10g fresh basil leaves, torn

For the pesto:
30g rocket
20g fresh flat-leaf parsley
10g fresh oregano
10g fresh basil
juice of ½ lemon
2 tbsp olive oil
fine sea salt and freshly ground
    black pepper

Why not try a different spin on this?

SWITCH IT

You can swap the rocket for baby spinach, kale or chard leaves.

Avoca Summer Harvest

Serves 4

Perfectly ripe strawberries make this summer salad extra sunny and special.

METHOD

First make the balsamic syrup by putting the vinegar and brown sugar in a small saucepan and bringing to the boil, then reduce the heat to medium-low and simmer for 5 to 10 minutes, stirring or swirling the pan occasionally, until thickened and syrupy. When it's ready, it should coat the back of a spoon. Allow to cool.

Toss the kale, salad leaves, beetroot and red onion together in a large bowl. Arrange on a serving dish, and scatter with strawberries, crumbled goat cheese and toasted flaked almonds.

Drizzle with the balsamic syrup and serve straightaway.

100g baby kale, chopped
100g mixed baby salad leaves
100g raw beetroot, peeled and grated
1 small red onion, halved and very thinly sliced
200g fresh strawberries, hulled and sliced
100g goat cheese, crumbled
40g toasted flaked almonds

For the balsamic syrup:
100ml balsamic vinegar
50g light brown sugar

Spring, Summer, Autumn, Winter...

SEASONAL

When they are in season, Wexford strawberries are our favourite.

Crunchy Rainbow Sesame Slaw

Serves 4

This vibrant, quick and easy slaw is aptly named, as it boasts almost every colour of the rainbow and brightens up any summer spread or barbecue.

METHOD

Make the dressing by whisking the maple syrup, red wine vinegar, sesame oil and a good pinch of salt and pepper together in a large bowl.

Add the cabbage, carrots, spring onions, fennel, radishes, edamame and chilli directly to the dressing in the bowl and toss to coat, then scatter the sesame seeds and coriander on top and toss again until just combined.

½ red cabbage, cored and
  shredded
2 carrots, peeled and grated
2 spring onions, thinly sliced
1 small fennel bulb, thinly sliced
10 radishes, thinly sliced
100g edamame beans
1 large fresh red chilli, deseeded
  and thinly sliced
1 tsp black sesame seeds
1 tsp white sesame seeds
20g fresh coriander, roughly
  chopped

For the sesame and maple dressing:
20ml maple syrup
20ml red wine vinegar
20ml sesame oil
fine sea salt and freshly ground
  black pepper

Avoca Quiche: The Basics

Our Basic Quiche Filling & Pastry

Makes 8 to 10 slices

Our trusty basic quiche recipe is the perfect base to add your favourite fillings to – we've put together a selection of recipes for you to choose from in the following pages.

FOR THE BASIC QUICHE FILLING

To make the basic filling, put the eggs, egg yolks, cream and the salt and pepper in a large bowl and whisk until combined. Set aside in the fridge until needed.

FOR THE SHORTCRUST PASTRY

To make the pastry, sift the flour into a bowl and rub in the butter until the mixture resembles fine breadcrumbs. Stir in the salt, then mix to a dough with the egg yolks and a little cold water if needed to bring it together. Shape into a flat disc rather than a ball, as this will make it easier to roll out the pastry later. Wrap in cling film and chill in the fridge for 30 minutes.

Preheat the oven to 180°C.

Lightly flour the base of a deep loose-bottomed 30cm tart tin or quiche dish. Roll out the pastry between two sheets of cling film so that you're not introducing any extra flour and so that the pastry doesn't stick. Remove the cling film, then use the rolling pin to lift the pastry into the tin. Press the pastry into the base and sides of the tin, allowing it to hang about 1cm over the edges. Crimp the edges if you like.

Place a sheet of non-stick baking paper onto the base, also allowing it to hang over the edges. Add a layer of ceramic baking beans or dried beans, rice or lentils and spread them out evenly. Bake the base in the preheated oven for 20 minutes, then carefully remove and discard the baking beans and paper. Return the base to the oven and bake for 5 to 10 minutes more, until golden brown and firm.

Remove from the oven and allow to cool on a wire rack before adding your quiche mixture. Choose one of our quiche filling recipes from the next few pages, or try your own combinations.

For the basic quiche filling:
5 large eggs
4 large egg yolks
250ml cream
¼ tsp fine sea salt
¼ tsp freshly ground black pepper

For the shortcrust pastry:
225g plain flour
150g butter, chilled and diced
½ tsp fine sea salt
1 to 2 egg yolks
a small splash of cold water,
    if needed

Our chefs let us in on a little secret...

CHEF'S TIP

Pop a marble rolling pin in the fridge 10 minutes before rolling the pastry to prevent it sticking.

Hot Smoked Salmon
with Leek, Garlic Potato & Dill

Makes 8 to 10 slices

METHOD

Make the basic quiche filling and pastry as per the recipes on page 100.

Preheat the oven to 180°C.

Melt the butter in a frying pan over a medium heat. Add the leek and cook for 5 to 6 minutes, until softened. Season lightly.

Combine the potato, garlic, salt and pepper and cream in a large bowl and mix well. Transfer to a baking dish and cover the top tightly with tin foil. Bake in the preheated oven for 20 minutes, until the potatoes are soft. Allow to cool slightly.

When the potatoes come out of the oven, reduce the temperature to 160°C.

Scatter the garlic potatoes evenly over the base of the quiche, then add the hot smoked salmon on top of the potatoes, followed by the leeks and dill. Place the tart tin or quiche dish on a baking tray (to make it easier to transfer the quiche to the oven), then pour over the basic quiche filling, leaving a small gap clear at the top so that it doesn't spill over the pastry. Cook in the oven for 45 minutes, until the eggs are firmly set and the quiche is golden.

Allow to cool in the dish on a wire rack for 30 minutes. Using a sharp knife, carefully cut the rough pastry down to the edges of the dish. Cut into wedges and serve warm or at room temperature.

For the basic quiche filling:
5 large eggs
4 large egg yolks
250ml cream
¼ tsp fine sea salt
¼ tsp freshly ground black
   pepper

For the shortcrust pastry:
225g plain flour
150g butter, chilled and diced
½ tsp fine sea salt
1 to 2 egg yolks
a small splash of cold water, if
   needed

For the filling:
30g butter
1 leek, white part only, thinly
   sliced
1 large potato, peeled and cut
   into 5mm-thick slices
1 garlic clove, minced
¼ tsp fine sea salt
¼ tsp freshly ground black
   pepper
150ml cream
150g hot smoked salmon,
   flaked
5g fresh dill, finely chopped

Spinach, Sun-dried Tomato, Basil & Feta

Makes 8 to 10 slices

METHOD

Make the basic quiche filling and pastry as per the recipes on page 100.

Preheat the oven to 160°C.

Heat the oil in a large frying pan over a medium heat. Add the spinach and cook, stirring, for 2 to 3 minutes, just until it has wilted down. Season lightly with salt and pepper.

Scatter the spinach, sun-dried tomatoes, feta and basil evenly over the quiche base. Place the tart tin or quiche dish on a baking tray (to make it easier to transfer the quiche to the oven), then pour over the basic quiche filling, leaving a small gap clear at the top so that it doesn't spill over the pastry. Cook in the oven for 45 minutes, until the eggs are firmly set and the quiche is golden.

Allow to cool in the dish on a wire rack for 30 minutes. Using a sharp knife, carefully cut the rough pastry down to the edges of the dish. Cut into wedges and serve warm or at room temperature.

For the basic quiche filling:
5 large eggs
4 large egg yolks
250ml cream
$\frac{1}{4}$ tsp fine sea salt
$\frac{1}{4}$ tsp freshly ground black
    pepper

For the shortcrust pastry:
225g plain flour
150g butter, chilled and
    diced
$\frac{1}{2}$ tsp fine sea salt
1 to 2 egg yolks
a small splash of cold
    water, if needed

For the filling:
1 tbsp rapeseed oil
120g baby spinach
120g sun-dried tomatoes
    in oil, roughly chopped
180g feta cheese,
    crumbled
15 fresh basil leaves, torn

Our chefs let us in on a little secret...

CHEF'S TIP

Feel free to use tins of different shapes and sizes, just note that cooking times may vary.

Smoked Bacon, Brie & Leek

Makes 8 to 10 slices

METHOD

Make the basic quiche filling and pastry as per the recipes on page 100.

Preheat the oven to 160°C.

Heat the butter and oil in a frying pan over a medium heat. Once the butter has melted, add the leeks and cook for 8 to 10 minutes, until softened.

Meanwhile, in a separate frying pan, fry the smoked bacon pieces until they are fully cooked.

Scatter the leeks, smoked bacon and Brie evenly over the quiche base. Place the tart tin or quiche dish on a baking tray (to make it easier to transfer the quiche to the oven), then pour over the basic quiche filling, leaving a small gap clear at the top so that it doesn't spill over the pastry. Cook in the oven for 45 minutes, until the eggs are firmly set and the quiche is golden.

Allow to cool in the dish on a wire rack for 30 minutes. Using a sharp knife, carefully cut the rough pastry down to the edges of the dish. Cut into wedges and serve warm or at room temperature.

For the basic quiche filling:
5 large eggs
4 large egg yolks
250ml cream
1/4 tsp fine sea salt
1/4 tsp freshly ground
   black pepper

For the shortcrust pastry:
225g plain flour
150g butter, chilled and
   diced
1/2 tsp fine sea salt
1 to 2 egg yolks
a small splash of cold
   water, if needed

For the filling:
40g butter
2 tbsp rapeseed oil
200g leek, thinly sliced
200g smoked bacon,
   chopped
150g Brie cheese, cut
   into 2cm pieces

Goat Cheese & Crispy Sage
with Onion Marmalade & Rosemary

Makes 8 to 10 slices

METHOD

Make the basic quiche filling and pastry as per the recipes on page 100.

Preheat the oven to 160°C.

Heat the oil in a small frying pan over a medium to high heat. When the oil is nice and hot, add the sage leaves and fry for only a few seconds, until they turn crisp and dark green. Gently remove them from the pan with a fork (be careful, as they'll have turned brittle now), transfer to a plate lined with kitchen paper and sprinkle with salt. Allow to cool, then chop.

Spread a layer of onion marmalade all over the bottom of the quiche. Scatter the goat cheese, rosemary and fried sage evenly over the base. Place the tart tin or quiche dish on a baking tray (to make it easier to transfer the quiche to the oven), then pour over the basic quiche filling.

Cook in the oven for 45 minutes, until the eggs are firmly set and the quiche is golden.

Allow to cool in the dish on a wire rack for 30 minutes. Using a sharp knife, carefully cut the rough pastry down to the edges of the dish. Cut into wedges and serve warm or at room temperature.

For the basic quiche filling:
5 large eggs
4 large egg yolks
250ml cream
¼ tsp fine sea salt
¼ tsp freshly ground
   black pepper

For the shortcrust pastry:
225g plain flour
150g butter, chilled and
   diced
½ tsp fine sea salt
1 to 2 egg yolks
a small splash of cold
   water, if needed

For the filling:
1 tbsp rapeseed oil
12g fresh sage leaves
a pinch of fine sea salt
150g shop-bought
   onion marmalade
170g goat cheese,
   crumbled
1 or 2 sprigs of fresh
   rosemary, finely
   chopped

Our chefs let us in on a little secret...

CHEF'S TIP

Feel free to use tins of different shapes and sizes, just note that cooking times may vary.

COMFORT FOOD

These are the meals that are like a big hug, hearty
food that's good for the soul and makes you
feel all warm and fuzzy. There's nothing quite
like a home-cooked meal and these recipes will
bring you comfort and happiness in spades. Best
enjoyed while you're wrapped up nice and cosy,
listening to the rain beat against the windows.

Food that makes
memories.

Creamy Chicken, Ham & Leek Bake

Serves 4 to 6

The epitome of comfort food. Warming and indulgent, you can swap out the crumble for a creamy mashed potato topping if you'd like to change things up.

METHOD

Preheat the oven to 180°C.

Bring the chicken stock to the boil, then reduce the heat to keep it simmering gently.

Melt half the butter in a separate large saucepan over a medium heat. When it's foaming, stir in the flour with a wooden spoon and cook for about 5 minutes to create a golden-brown roux.

Add half the hot stock to the roux and cook for 3 to 4 minutes, whisking continuously, then pour in the remaining stock and cook for 3 to 4 minutes more, still whisking until thickened and smooth. Remove from the heat and whisk in the cream and mustard, ensuring there are no lumps of roux in the sauce. Remove the pan from the heat and set aside.

Heat the oil in a frying pan over a medium heat. Add the leek and cook for about 5 minutes, until softened.

Put the cooked chicken and ham in a large bowl with 1 tablespoon of the parsley, then pour in the white sauce and mix well. Season to taste, but go easy on the salt as the stock, ham and butter are already salty. Transfer to a baking dish and spread it out evenly. A 25cm square Pyrex dish is ideal but use whatever you have.

Melt the remaining butter in a frying pan over a medium heat. Add the breadcrumbs and the remaining tablespoon of parsley and toss to coat the breadcrumbs in the butter, then scatter this over the chicken and ham along with the grated Cheddar.

Bake in the preheated oven for 10 to 12 minutes, until the breadcrumb topping is golden brown and the cheese has melted. Serve straight to the table.

600ml chicken stock
100g butter
50g plain flour
175ml cream
2 tbsp wholegrain mustard
2 tbsp rapeseed oil
1 large leek, white part only, sliced
500g cooked chicken fillets, cut into bite-sized chunks
250g cooked ham, cut into bite-sized chunks
2 tbsp chopped fresh flat-leaf parsley
150g fresh breadcrumbs
40g grated white Cheddar cheese
fine sea salt and freshly ground black pepper

Pork Meatballs
with Spaghetti al Burro

Serves 4 to 6

Cheese, cream and carbs – this dish is next-level decadence. Everyone around the table will be members of the Clean Plate Club after this one!

METHOD

Preheat the oven to 220°C. Line a baking tray with non-stick baking paper.

To make the meatballs, put the onion, carrot and celery in a food processor and pulse until finely chopped, but don't blend it to a purée. Alternatively, you could finely dice the veg by hand.

Put the chopped veg in a large bowl with all the other meatball ingredients and season generously with salt and pepper. Mix until everything is well combined, then form into large meatballs about 70g each. You should get 12 large meatballs.

Place the meatballs on the lined baking tray and bake in the oven for 15 to 20 minutes, until cooked through (if you have a digital meat thermometer, they should have an internal temperature of 75°C).

Meanwhile, cook the spaghetti in boiling salted water for 8 to 10 minutes, until al dente, or according to the packet instructions. Reserve a mugful (250ml) of the pasta cooking water before you drain the spaghetti.

Add the spaghetti to the softened butter in a large saucepan over a medium heat and cook for 1 minute to let the butter start to melt. Add three-quarters of the grated cheeses, then add the pasta cooking water a little at a time, stirring until you get a smooth sauce. Season lightly with salt, as the butter and cheese are already salty, but add plenty of freshly ground black pepper.

To serve, divide the pasta between wide, shallow bowls and add the meatballs on top, then scatter over the remaining grated cheese.

½ small onion, roughly chopped
1 small carrot, peeled and
  roughly chopped
1 celery stalk, roughly chopped
2 garlic cloves, finely chopped
1 large egg, beaten
450g pork mince
200g grated Parmesan cheese
200g fresh breadcrumbs
70g pine nuts
40g grated Pecorino Romano
  cheese
50ml cream
2 tbsp finely chopped fresh flat-
  leaf parsley
¼ tsp ground nutmeg

For the spaghetti al burro:
500g spaghetti
150g butter, cubed and at room
  temperature
100g grated Parmesan cheese
30g grated Pecorino Romano
  cheese
fine sea salt and freshly ground
  black pepper

Why not try a different spin on this?

SWITCH IT

You can leave the meatballs out – the spaghetti al burro is a fantastic pasta dish on its own.

Good Mood Veggie Chilli

Serves 4 to 6

Aptly named, this deliciously smoky chilli never fails to put a smile on your face. It's perfect for burritos, tacos, nachos, rice bowls or just on its own.

METHOD

Soak the lentils, bulghur and barley in cold water for 1 hour, then drain.

Heat the oil in a large heavy-based saucepan or casserole dish over a low heat. Add the onion and pepper and cook for about 10 minutes, until softened and the onion is translucent. Add the garlic, ginger and spices and cook for a further 3 to 4 minutes, until fragrant.

Increase the heat slightly and add the wine. Let it bubble up for a few minutes, stirring to deglaze the pan, then add the passata and stock along with the soaked lentils, bulghur and barley and the chickpeas. Simmer gently for 25 to 30 minutes, until the lentils and grains are soft and plump. You may need to add extra stock as it simmers and the grains absorb the liquid – just keep topping it up as needed.

Season well with salt and pepper, then stir in the chopped fresh coriander. Bring the pot straight to the table and serve with some steamed brown rice and a dollop of Greek yogurt, chunky guacamole, a squeeze of fresh lime and a few fresh coriander leaves.

50g Puy lentils
50g beluga lentils (or another 50g of Puy lentils)
50g bulghur wheat
50g pearl barley
2 tbsp rapeseed oil
1 large onion, finely diced
1 red pepper, diced
4 garlic cloves, finely chopped
1 tbsp peeled and grated ginger
1 tsp smoked chipotle chilli flakes
1 tsp smoked paprika
1 tsp ground cumin
150ml white wine
1 x 500g carton of tomato passata
250ml vegetable stock, plus extra if needed
1 x 400g tin of chickpeas, drained and rinsed
20g fresh coriander, chopped, plus whole leaves to garnish
fine sea salt and freshly ground black pepper

To serve:
steamed brown rice
Greek yogurt
guacamole (page 214)
a squeeze of lime

Smoky Chicken & Chorizo

Serves 4

There's a delicious heat in this rich and comforting dish. Ideal for rustling up on a winter's night, who doesn't love a one-pot wonder?

METHOD

Trim off any excess skin from the chicken thighs and put a wide, shallow, heavy-based casserole dish over a medium-high heat without any oil. When the pan is nice and hot, reduce the heat to medium and add the chicken thighs, skin side down, to render out the fat. Cook for 5 minutes without moving them around, then flip them over and cook for 5 minutes on the other side too, until nicely browned. Remove from the pan and set aside on a plate.

Add the chorizo and cook for 5 minutes, until it has released its oil into the pan and crisped up a bit. Using a slotted spoon, transfer the chorizo to the plate with the chicken. Pour off all the oil that has been released from the chicken and chorizo, as there will be a lot of fat in the pan now, then add 1 or 2 tablespoons back in.

Preheat the oven to 180°C.

Add the onion, carrots and celery and season with salt and pepper. Cook for about 10 minutes, until softened. Add the garlic, bay leaf, smoked paprika, oregano, rosemary, cumin, thyme, chilli flakes and saffron and cook for 1 or 2 minutes more, just until fragrant.

Pour in the wine and let it bubble up for 1 or 2 minutes, stirring to deglaze the pan, then stir in the passata and add the browned chicken thighs and chorizo back in. Bring to the boil, then reduce the heat to medium-low, cover the casserole dish and transfer to the oven for 25 to 30 minutes, until the chicken is fully cooked.

Near the end of the cooking time, stir in the cannellini beans and olives to warm them through.

Taste and adjust the seasoning, then scatter over the chopped parsley. Serve straight to the table.

8 chicken thighs, bone in
  and skin on
100g dry-cured chorizo, diced
1 onion, chopped
1 large carrot, peeled and diced
2 celery stalks, diced
3 large garlic cloves, crushed
1 bay leaf
1½ tbsp smoked paprika
1 tbsp chopped fresh oregano
  (or 1 tsp dried oregano)
1 tsp finely chopped fresh rosemary
1 tsp ground cumin
½ tsp chopped fresh thyme
¼ to ½ tsp chilli flakes, depending
  on how spicy you like your food
a pinch of saffron
200ml white wine
1 x 700g jar of tomato passata
1 x 400g tin of cannellini beans,
  drained and rinsed
80g black Kalamata olives, pitted
  and halved
1 tbsp chopped fresh flat-leaf
  parsley
fine sea salt and freshly ground
  black pepper

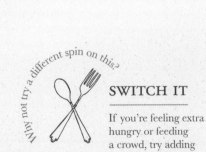

Why not try a different spin on this?

SWITCH IT

If you're feeling extra hungry or feeding a crowd, try adding diced boiled potatoes at the end.

Fish Pie
Topped with Sweet Potato Champ

Serves 4 to 6

Spoiler alert: we've put a delicious twist on this classic dish by making it with a velouté sauce and topping it with a sweet potato and Parmesan champ.

METHOD

Preheat the oven to 180°C.

Fill a saucepan with water and bring to the boil, then reduce the heat to medium, add the smoked haddock, salmon and cod and poach for 8 to 10 minutes, until cooked through. Use a slotted spoon to remove the fish from the poaching water, then break it all into large chunks and set aside.

Meanwhile, to make the velouté, start by making a roux. Melt the butter in a large saucepan over a medium heat (this is the pan that you'll be cooking all the sauce in eventually). Add the flour and stir to make a paste. Cook for a few minutes, until golden. Remove the pan from the heat and set aside.

Heat the rapeseed oil in a separate large saucepan over a medium heat. Add the onion, carrot, celery, fennel and leek and cook for about 10 minutes, until softened. Pour in the wine and increase the heat to high to let the wine bubble up and reduce a bit, stirring to deglaze the pan, then pour in the stock.

Transfer the hot vegetable and stock mixture into the saucepan with the roux and put that pan back over a high heat. Bring to the boil, stirring constantly, then reduce the heat and simmer for 3 to 4 minutes, until thickened. Remove the pan from the heat and blitz with a hand-held blender into a smooth sauce, then stir in the cream along with the poached fish. Set aside.

Continues ...

For the fish:
300g smoked haddock
300g salmon
300g cod

For the velouté:
50g butter
50g plain flour
1 tbsp rapeseed oil
½ medium onion, chopped
½ medium carrot, peeled and
    chopped
1 celery stalk, chopped
⅓ fennel bulb, chopped
¼ leek, white part only, chopped
100ml white wine
400ml good-quality shellfish or
    fish stock
100ml cream

For the sweet potato champ topping:
900g sweet potatoes, peeled and
    cut into large cubes
900g Rooster potatoes, peeled
    and cut into large cubes
50g butter
75ml cream
75g grated Parmesan cheese
4 spring onions, finely diced
fine sea salt and freshly ground
    black pepper

Our chefs let us in on a little secret...

CHEF'S TIP

Ask your fishmonger to remove all the skin from the fish for you.

METHOD CONTINUED

To make the sweet potato champ topping, boil or steam the sweet potatoes and Roosters for 10 to 15 minutes, until cooked through. Mash until smooth with the butter, cream and half the grated Parmesan, then stir in the chopped spring onions and season well with salt and pepper.

You can either bake the fish pie in individual ovenproof dishes or one medium-sized baking dish (you don't want to use a dish that's too large or you won't have enough champ topping to cover the pie). Ladle the filling to within 3cm of the top of the dish. Add the sweet potato mash on top, spreading it out in an even layer, then scatter over the remaining grated Parmesan.

Cook in the preheated oven for 8 to 10 minutes, until the topping is golden brown and the filling is piping hot. Allow to stand for 5 minutes before serving straight to the table.

One of our foodie favourites...

TASTE TIP

Take this dish up a notch by adding prawns.

Irish Mac 'n' Cheese

Serves 6

Lifting this golden, bubbling mac 'n' cheese from the oven will have you feeling almost giddy. It's made even more glorious with crunchy garlic and thyme croutons.

METHOD

Preheat the oven to 180°C.

To make the sauce, melt the butter in a saucepan over a medium heat. When it's foaming, stir in the flour with a wooden spoon and cook for about 5 minutes to create a golden-brown roux. Pour in the milk and bring it up to a simmer, whisking continuously for a few minutes to thicken.

Add most of the grated cheeses (save some to scatter on top at the end) along with the parsley, mustard and nutmeg and season well with salt and pepper to taste. Remove from the heat and set aside.

To make the croutons, melt the butter and oil together over a medium heat. Add the garlic and thyme, then add the baguette pieces and toss to coat. Set aside.

Bring a large pot of salted water to the boil. Add the macaroni and cook for 8 minutes – it should not be fully cooked, as it will finish cooking in the oven. Drain.

Stir the cooked pasta into the cheese sauce, then transfer to a baking dish. Top with the chunky croutons and scatter over the reserved cheese. Bake in the preheated oven for 20 to 25 minutes, until the croutons are golden and the pasta bake is bubbling. Serve straight to the table.

30g butter
30g plain flour
500ml milk
85g grated Saint Gall cheese
  (or Comté or Gruyère)
85g grated Hegarty's Cheddar
  cheese (or a mature Cheddar)
2 tbsp chopped fresh flat-leaf
  parsley
1 tbsp Dijon mustard
¼ tsp ground nutmeg
400g macaroni pasta

For the garlic and herb croutons:
20g butter
4 tsp olive oil
1 garlic clove, crushed
1 tbsp fresh thyme leaves
¼ large baguette, roughly torn
  into large bite-sized pieces
fine sea salt and freshly ground
  black pepper

Autumn Risotto
with Squash & Sage

Serves 4

A bowl of risotto is the perfect comfort food. The sweetness of roasted squash mixed with the earthy sage and nutty Parmesan are a match made in heaven. Add strips of smoked streaky bacon and toasted pine nuts if you're feeling fancy.

METHOD

Preheat the oven to 180°C.

Scatter the diced butternut squash over a baking tray, drizzle with the oil and season lightly with salt and pepper. Roast in the preheated oven for 20 to 25 minutes, until soft.

Divide the roasted squash in half. Blend one half to a smooth purée and keep the other half as it is to mix through the risotto for added texture.

Meanwhile, put the stock in a saucepan and bring to the boil, then reduce the heat to a simmer to keep it hot.

Melt the butter in a heavy-based saucepan or casserole dish over a medium heat. Add the onion, sage and a pinch of salt and cook for about 10 minutes, until softened and transparent but not coloured. Add the rice, star anise, lemon zest, turmeric and nutmeg, stirring to coat the rice in the butter. Cook for 1 or 2 minutes, until you start to see the rice turning transparent.

Add the wine, stirring to deglaze the pan. Cook gently for 3 to 4 minutes, until the wine has all been absorbed by the rice. Add the hot stock one ladleful at a time, stirring constantly until all the stock has been absorbed before adding the next ladleful. It will take up to 20 minutes to cook the risotto, stirring all the time to release the starch from the rice and give the risotto its deliciously creamy texture. Risotto is meant to be served al dente, so you might not need all the stock.

Stir in the butternut squash purée and roasted cubes and cook for 1 or 2 minutes to warm them through. Remove the pan from the heat and stir in the Parmesan and parsley. Serve immediately.

1 large butternut squash, peeled and diced
1 tbsp olive oil
1 litre vegetable stock
50g butter
1 medium onion, diced
2 tbsp finely chopped fresh sage
300g risotto rice (Carnaroli or Vialone Nano are the best)
1 star anise
1 tsp lemon zest
½ tsp ground turmeric
½ tsp ground nutmeg
150ml white wine
120g grated Parmesan cheese
2 tbsp chopped fresh flat-leaf parsley
fine sea salt and freshly ground black pepper

Roasted Veggie Lasagne

Serves 4 to 6

Packed with veggie goodness, the creamy green béchamel sauce gives this lasagne a tasty and colourful twist. Even better, you can add any extra veg you need to use up and they'll only make it even more delicious.

METHOD

Preheat the oven to 200°C.

Place all the peppers on baking tray, drizzle with a little of the olive oil and season with salt and pepper. Roast for 10 to 15 minutes, until softened. Set aside and reduce the oven temperature to 160°C.

Meanwhile, to start making the béchamel, pour the milk into a medium-sized saucepan. Add the onion and nutmeg and bring to the boil over a low heat, keeping a close eye on it to make sure the milk doesn't boil up and over the sides of the pan. As soon as it comes to the boil, remove the pan from the heat and set it aside to allow the flavours to infuse the milk.

To return to preparing the vegetables, heat the remaining olive oil in a large heavy-based saucepan over a medium heat. Add the onion and garlic and cook for 2 to 3 minutes, until the onion is starting to soften and the garlic is fragrant. Add the aubergine and cook for 3 to 4 minutes, until starting to soften, then add the courgettes and cook for a further 2 minutes. Add the cherry tomatoes, passata, roasted peppers and chilli flakes and cook for 5 minutes to bring everything together. Season to taste with salt and pepper, then stir in the basil and parsley. Set aside while you finish making the béchamel.

Place the spinach in a hot dry frying pan over a medium heat. Cook until it has wilted right down, then allow to cool. Squeeze out the excess water, then chop finely and set aside.

Continues ...

For the spinach béchamel:
550ml milk
1 small onion, quartered
¼ tsp grated nutmeg
50g baby spinach
45g butter
45g plain flour
2 tbsp grated Parmesan cheese

For the vegetables:
1 large red pepper, cut into 8 pieces
1 large yellow pepper, cut into 8 pieces
1 large green pepper, cut into 8 pieces
5 tbsp olive oil
1 medium onion, roughly chopped
4 garlic cloves, finely chopped
1 medium aubergine, cut into 3cm chunks
1 medium courgette, cut into 3cm chunks
12 cherry tomatoes, halved
1 x 700g jar of tomato passata
½ tsp chilli flakes
4 tbsp shredded fresh basil
2 tbsp chopped fresh flat-leaf parsley
fine sea salt and freshly ground black pepper

To assemble:
80g grated Parmesan cheese
4 tbsp chopped fresh flat-leaf parsley
200g fresh lasagne sheets

METHOD CONTINUED

Melt the butter in a saucepan over a medium heat. When it's foaming, stir in the flour with a wooden spoon and cook for about 5 minutes to create a golden-brown roux.

Strain the milk through a fine-mesh sieve and discard the onion, then add the milk to the roux and bring it up to a simmer, whisking continuously for a few minutes to thicken. Add the chopped cooked spinach and the Parmesan, stirring until the cheese has melted. Taste and adjust the seasoning with salt and pepper.

To assemble, mix the Parmesan cheese and parsley together.

In a deep baking dish, build up the layers as follows: vegetables, lasagne sheets, béchamel, Parmesan and parsley mixture. Repeat the layers until everything has been used up, finishing with a layer of béchamel with the Parmesan and parsley mix scattered on top of it.

The lasagne can be made up to two days in advance up to this point and kept in the fridge until you need it. Just bring it back to room temperature before baking in the oven.

Place the baking dish on a baking tray to catch any drips and cook in the preheated oven (which should be at 160°C now) for 30 to 35 minutes. You will know the lasagne is cooked when a knife can easily slide through the lasagne sheets straight through to the bottom. If the lasagne sheets still seem a little too al dente, cook for another 5 minutes.

Allow to stand for at least 10 minutes before cutting into slices to serve.

Irish Spring Lamb Stew

Serves 6

Ideal for a springtime gathering, this seasonal dish
puts on a show.

METHOD

Preheat the oven to 180°C.

Put the whole, unpeeled garlic cloves on a square of tin foil and
wrap it up into a parcel, making sure it's tightly sealed. Roast
the garlic in the oven for 15 minutes, until soft. Open the foil
packet and allow to cool slightly, then squeeze the roasted garlic
out of its skins with the back of a knife. Set aside.

Heat 3 tablespoons of the oil in a large heavy-based casserole
dish over a high heat. When the pan is smoking hot, season
the diced lamb with salt and pepper. Working in batches so
that you don't crowd the pan, add the lamb and cook just
until browned. Use a slotted spoon to transfer to a bowl, then
pour off all the fat and oil in the pan.

Reduce the heat to medium and add the remaining 2
tablespoons of oil, then add the onion, carrots, celery and a
pinch of salt and cook for about 10 minutes, until softened.
Add the wine and let it bubble up for a minute or two, stirring
to deglaze the pan. Add the lamb back to the pan along with
the roasted garlic, thyme and rosemary sprigs, bay leaves,
stock and lemon zest. Cover the pan and bring to the boil,
then transfer to the oven and cook for 45 minutes, until the
lamb is tender.

Add the baby potatoes to the lamb. Return the casserole dish
to the oven and cook, still covered, for 30 minutes more, until
the potatoes are completely cooked through.

Meanwhile, cook the barley separately in a pan of boiling
water for 25 to 30 minutes, until tender. Drain, then add the
cooked pearl barley to the lamb along with the parsley, mint
and lemon juice. Return to the oven to cook for a further
2 to 3 minutes, then taste and adjust the seasoning.

To serve, bring the stew straight to the table along with plenty
of good crusty bread to let everyone help themselves.

1 head of garlic
5 tbsp rapeseed oil
850g diced lamb shoulder
1 large onion, diced
2 carrots, peeled and diced
3 celery stalks, diced
70ml white wine
5 sprigs of fresh thyme
2 sprigs of fresh rosemary
2 bay leaves
750ml vegetable stock
zest of 1 small lemon and 2 tbsp
   juice
300g baby potatoes, halved or
   quartered
60g pearl barley
4 tsp chopped fresh flat-leaf
   parsley
4 tsp chopped fresh mint
fine sea salt and freshly ground
   black pepper

To serve:
crusty bread

SEASONAL
Swap the roast garlic
for wild garlic when
it's in season from
March to May.

Beetroot & Feta Burgers
with Guacamole

Serves 4 to 6

A firm favourite with veggies and meat eaters alike!

METHOD

Preheat the oven to 200°C. Line a baking tray with non-stick baking paper.

Put the grated beetroot, feta, oats, paprika, dill and a good pinch of salt and pepper in a large bowl. Using your hands, work the mix until it comes together – the feta will bind it all together.

Divide the mix into four burgers. Place on the lined tray and cook in the preheated oven for about 20 minutes, until heated through and firm to the touch.

To serve, place each burger on a bun base. Top with cucumber slices, rocket and guacamole, sandwiching everything together with the bun lid.

400g raw beetroot, peeled
    and grated
200g feta cheese
100g porridge oats
1 tsp smoked paprika
2 tbsp chopped fresh dill
fine sea salt and freshly
    ground black pepper

To serve:
4 burger buns or
    Waterford blaas
cucumber slices
rocket
guacamole (page 214)

One of our foodie favourites...

TASTE TIP

Mix some chipotle chilli paste with soy yogurt for a delicious burger sauce.

Red Lentil, Cauliflower & Coconut Dahl

Serves 4 to 6

Endlessly satisfying and warming yet incredibly simple, our favourite one-pot wonder is perfect for any night of the week. If you like your dahl to be extra creamy, use full-fat coconut milk.

METHOD

Melt the coconut oil in a large heavy-based saucepan or casserole dish over a medium heat. Add the mustard seeds and cook for about 2 minutes, until the seeds start to pop.

Add the onion and a large pinch of salt and cook for 10 minutes, until softened. Add the garlic and cook for 1 minute more, just until fragrant. Stir in the ground coriander, turmeric, ground cumin and chilli flakes and cook for another minute.

Stir in the cauliflower, lentils, coconut milk, passata and water. Bring to the boil, then reduce the heat and simmer for 20 to 25 minutes, stirring often, until the lentils and cauliflower are cooked through and tender. Add the spinach and chopped fresh coriander at the end, stirring until the spinach has wilted down. Stir in the lemon juice and season to taste with salt and pepper.

Serve with plain boiled basmati rice (or brown rice for a healthier option) and warm naan or flatbreads. This keeps well in the fridge for up to three days and it freezes well too.

4 tbsp coconut oil
2 tbsp mustard seeds
1 large onion, diced
4 garlic cloves, finely chopped
2 tsp ground coriander
2 tsp ground turmeric
1 tsp ground cumin
$\frac{1}{2}$ to 1 tsp chilli flakes, to taste
1 medium head of cauliflower, cut into small bite-sized florets
180g dried red lentils
1 x 400ml tin of coconut milk
400ml tomato passata
600ml water
75g baby spinach
2 tbsp chopped fresh coriander
juice of 1 lemon
fine sea salt and freshly ground black pepper

To serve:
plain boiled basmati rice
warm naan or flatbreads (page 70)

PASTA

Delicious, simple, versatile, wonderful pasta.
There really is a perfect pasta dish for every
occasion, whether you need a quick and easy
midweek meal, a recipe for a romantic candlelit
dinner or a dish for a dinner party.

Bubbling pots
& *twirling forks.*

Sausage Ragù

Serves 4 to 6

A delicious alternative to the more traditional beef ragù, this sausage and Pecorino version is sure to become a firm favourite. Rich and decadent with a hint of creaminess – feel free to add more chilli flakes if you want to turn up the heat. Penne pasta works well with this sauce, but any pasta shape you have at home will do the trick.

METHOD

Heat the oil in a large, deep, heavy-based sauté pan or a wide, shallow casserole dish over a medium heat. Add the sausage meat, fennel seeds and chilli flakes and cook for 6 to 8 minutes, until browned, breaking up the sausage meat with a wooden spoon as it cooks.

Reduce the heat to low, then add the onion, carrot, celery and a pinch of salt and cook for 8 to 10 minutes, until softened. Add the garlic and cook for 1 minute more, just until fragrant.

Add the bay leaf and wine, letting the wine bubble up and stirring to deglaze the pan. Simmer for 3 or 4 minutes, until the wine has reduced by half. Stir in the passata and season well with salt and pepper. Cook on a low simmer for 15 minutes.

Add the cream, parsley and lemon zest and bring back to a simmer for a further 5 minutes.

Meanwhile, cook the pasta in a large saucepan of boiling salted water for 8 to 9 minutes, until al dente. Reserve a mugful of the cooking water, then drain the pasta. Add the cooked pasta to the ragù, tossing to coat. Add 5 or 6 tablespoons of the reserved pasta water to thin the sauce a bit.

To serve, divide between wide, shallow pasta bowls and top with freshly grated Pecorino.

2 tbsp olive oil
300g Toulouse or Italian-style pork sausage meat, removed from its casings
2 tsp fennel seeds
½ tsp chilli flakes
1 medium onion, diced
1 small carrot, peeled and diced
2 celery stalks, diced
4 garlic cloves, finely chopped
1 bay leaf
100ml white wine
1 x 700g jar of tomato passata
100ml cream
4 tbsp chopped fresh flat-leaf parsley
1 tsp lemon zest
500g penne
4 tbsp grated Pecorino cheese
fine sea salt and freshly ground black pepper

Homemade Gnocchi

Serves 4

Homemade gnocchi is delicious when made fresh and
Irish potatoes work really well. It's also a fantastic way to
use up leftover mashed potatoes. We've included two of
our favourite ways to serve gnocchi: a sweet and smoky
version made with chorizo and roast Hokkaido squash and
a decadent version that's perfect for autumn entertaining
served with Crozier Blue cheese, spinach and walnuts.

750g cooked mashed
   potatoes
150g '00' or strong white
   flour, plus extra for
   dusting
1 egg, beaten
½ tsp fine sea salt

METHOD

Mix the mashed potatoes, flour, egg and salt together in a
large bowl, then tip it out onto a lightly floured countertop
and knead gently until well combined, taking care not to
overmix. Using your hands, roll the dough into a long snake
shape until it's a little over 2cm thick. Cut into pieces 1cm
long, then use the back of a fork to gently roll each piece of
gnocchi. This gives the gnocchi those little indents that help
the sauce to stick to it, but it's not an essential step.

Bring two separate pots of salted water to the boil (we use
two pots so as not to overcrowd them and risk the gnocchi
sticking together). Add the gnocchi. When they have risen
to the top of the water, cook for a further 1 or 2 minutes,
then drain.

Toss with a few knobs of melted butter and season
generously with salt and pepper to enjoy as a simple supper
or make one of the following variations.

GNOCCHI WITH CROZIER BLUE, SPINACH & WALNUTS

Serves 4

Make the basic gnocchi as per the recipe.

Put the cream in a large saucepan and bring to the boil, taking care that the cream doesn't boil up and over the sides of the pan. As soon as it comes to the boil, reduce the heat, add the blue cheese and stir until it has melted and the sauce has thickened. Remove the pan from the heat, stir in the spinach, walnuts and sage and season to taste with salt and pepper.

Add the cooked gnocchi to the sauce and toss to coat. To serve, divide between warmed pasta bowls and scatter some extra walnuts and Crozier Blue on top.

1 batch of homemade gnocchi (page 143)
300ml cream
125g Crozier Blue cheese, plus extra to serve
100g baby spinach
50g chopped walnuts, plus extra to serve
1 tsp finely chopped fresh sage
fine sea salt and freshly ground black pepper

GNOCCHI WITH CHORIZO & ROAST HOKKAIDO SQUASH

Serves 4

Make the basic gnocchi as per the recipe.

Preheat the oven to 180°C.

Place the squash wedges on a baking tray and drizzle with the smoked rapeseed oil, then scatter over the sage, rosemary and thyme, season with salt and pepper and toss to coat. Roast in the preheated oven for 25 to 30 minutes, until tender. Allow to cool, then cut into 2cm pieces.

Put the whole, unpeeled garlic cloves on a square of tin foil and wrap it up into a parcel, making sure it's tightly sealed. Roast the garlic in the oven alongside the squash for 15 minutes, until soft. Open the foil packet and allow to cool slightly, then squeeze the roasted garlic out of its skins with the back of a knife. Set aside.

Meanwhile, heat the olive oil in a large frying pan over a medium heat. Add the chorizo and shallots and cook for 10 to 12 minutes more, until the shallots have softened and the chorizo has released its oil. Stir in the roasted squash and the roasted garlic paste.

Add the cooked gnocchi to the pan, tossing gently over a low heat until combined. Add the basil and toss one more time, then divide between warmed pasta bowls and serve with some Pecorino Romano cheese grated on top.

1 batch of homemade gnocchi (page 143)
1 Hokkaido or butternut squash, cut into wedges (there's no need to peel the Hokkaido squash but do peel a butternut)
2 tbsp smoked rapeseed oil
1 tbsp finely chopped fresh sage
1 tbsp finely chopped fresh rosemary
1 tbsp finely chopped fresh thyme
4 garlic cloves, unpeeled and left whole
2 tbsp olive oil
250g dry-cured Spanish chorizo, diced
8 shallots, chopped
8 fresh basil leaves, shredded
freshly grated Pecorino Romano cheese
fine sea salt and freshly ground black pepper

Mushroom & Bacon Creamy Fettuccine

Serves 4

This rich, creamy sauce has been one of our most-loved food market staples for years.

METHOD

Heat the oil in a large frying pan over a medium heat. Add the bacon lardons and fry until golden-brown. Use a slotted spoon to transfer to a plate lined with kitchen paper to drain, leaving the oil and any fat that rendered out of the bacon in the pan.

Add the butter to the pan and allow to melt, then reduce the heat to low. Add the onion, garlic and a pinch of salt and cook for about 5 minutes, then add the mushrooms and thyme and cook for another 10 minutes, until the onions and mushrooms have softened right down.

Cook the fettuccine in a large pot of boiling salted water for 10 to 12 minutes or according to the packet instructions, until al dente. Drain.

While the pasta is cooking, add the bacon back to the pan, then stir in the cream and simmer for 5 minutes. Add the fontina cheese and simmer for another 2 or 3 minutes to let the cheese melt. Season with freshly ground black pepper – the sauce should already be salty enough from the bacon and cheese, but if not, add a pinch of salt to taste. Add the cooked fettuccine to the sauce and toss to coat.

To serve, divide between warmed pasta bowls and top with the grated Parmesan.

1 tbsp rapeseed oil
220g bacon lardons
40g butter
1 medium onion, finely diced
4 garlic cloves, finely chopped
220g chestnut mushrooms, sliced
1 tsp chopped fresh thyme
400g fettuccine
350ml cream
30g fontina cheese, diced
20g grated Parmesan cheese
fine sea salt and freshly ground
    black pepper

Spaghetti al Limone

Serves 4 to 6

Easy, breezy and elegant, spaghetti al limone makes a beautifully simple summertime meal, best enjoyed al fresco. Because there are so few ingredients, try to use the best quality you can get. You can also make this dish with fresh tagliarini, which is a thinner version of tagliatelle.

METHOD

Put the cream and lemon zest in a large heavy-based saucepan over a medium-high heat. Bring to the boil, then reduce the heat to low and simmer for 2 minutes. Stirring continuously, add the butter 1 tablespoon at a time, waiting 30 to 45 seconds before adding the next tablespoon – the butter should be completely melted into the cream before you add more. The sauce will now be rich, glossy and emulsified. Set aside.

Cook the spaghetti in a large pot of boiling salted water for 9 to 11 minutes or according to the packet instructions, until al dente. Reserve a mugful of the pasta water before you drain the pasta.

Add half of the pasta water to the cream sauce and return to a simmer. Season generously with salt and pepper.

Turn the heat back down to low, add the cooked spaghetti to the sauce and toss to coat. Add the Parmesan 1 tablespoon at a time, just like you did with the butter, again waiting for 30 to 45 seconds before adding the next tablespoon. If the sauce is getting too stiff, add a little more of the pasta water to loosen it. Once all the Parmesan has been incorporated, pour in the lemon juice and toss once more.

To serve, divide between warmed pasta bowls and top with a little more freshly grated Parmesan.

225ml cream
2 organic unwaxed lemons
(zest of 2, juice of 1)
100g butter
500g spaghetti
150g grated Parmesan cheese,
plus extra to serve
fine sea salt and freshly
ground black pepper

Prawn & Chorizo Linguine

Serves 4 to 6

This prawn and chorizo linguine packs a punch when it comes to flavour and is as simple as it is delicious.

METHOD

Cook the linguine in a large pot of boiling salted water for 10 to 12 minutes or according to the packet instructions, until al dente. Drain.

While the pasta is cooking, heat the oil in a large frying pan over a medium heat. Add the chorizo and cook for a few minutes to release its oil. Use a slotted spoon to transfer to a plate lined with kitchen paper to drain.

Add the courgette to the oil left behind in the pan and cook for about 5 minutes, until it starts to colour, then add the cherry tomatoes and prawns. Just when the prawns are starting to turn pink, add the garlic and smoked paprika and cook for 1 to 2 minutes more.

Add the chorizo back to the pan along with the butter, wine and the lemon zest and juice. Let it all bubble up and reduce to form a sauce. Mix in the parsley and dill, then taste and adjust the seasoning with salt and pepper.

Add the cooked linguine to the pan, tossing to combine everything together. Divide between warmed pasta bowls and serve immediately.

500g linguine
2 tbsp olive oil
270g dry-cured chorizo, thinly sliced
1 large courgette, diced into 2cm cubes
8 cherry tomatoes, halved
500g large raw prawns, shelled and deveined
3 garlic cloves, crushed
1 tbsp smoked paprika
3 tbsp butter
100ml white wine
zest and juice of $\frac{1}{2}$ lemon
2 tbsp chopped fresh flat-leaf parsley
2 tbsp chopped fresh dill
fine sea salt and freshly ground black pepper

When writing your shopping list...

SHOPPING

For a tasty midweek treat add some frozen tiger prawns to your list. They're a great substitute if you don't have time to pop to your local fishmonger.

Baked Pasta Shells
with Spinach & Ricotta

Serves 4

Warming nutmeg meets mild, creamy ricotta cheese to
create a delicious filling that's generously stuffed into
oversized pasta shells. Finished with a light and crunchy
breadcrumb topping, this is a recipe you'll come back to
again and again.

METHOD

Preheat the oven to 170°C.

Bring a large pot of heavily salted water to the boil. Add the
pasta shells and cook for no more than 9 minutes – you want
them to be undercooked at this stage. Drain and cool them
down by running cold water over them. Drain again, then
drizzle with a little bit of oil to stop the shells sticking together.
Set aside.

Heat the oil in a large frying pan over a medium heat. Add the
spinach and cook for 1 or 2 minutes, just until it has wilted.
Remove the pan from the heat and allow the spinach to cool,
then squeeze out any moisture and roughly chop it.

Put the chopped spinach in a large bowl with the ricotta,
yogurt, Parmesan, garlic, lemon zest, basil and nutmeg and
mix to combine. Season to taste with salt and pepper.

Pour half the tomato passata over the bottom of a large
baking dish and season it with salt and pepper. Stuff each shell
with the ricotta and spinach mixture, then add the shells to
the dish on top of the sauce, stuffed side facing up. Once all
the shells have been filled and added to the dish, pour over the
remaining passata and another pinch of salt and pepper.

Mix together the breadcrumbs, Parmesan and thyme in
a small bowl, then pour over the melted butter and toss
to combine. Sprinkle this over the top of the pasta, then
bake in the preheated oven for 25 to 30 minutes, until the
breadcrumbs are golden and the pasta is bubbling.

Bring the dish straight to the table to serve family style.

250g conchiglioni (jumbo pasta
   shells)
1 tbsp rapeseed oil, plus extra
   for drizzling
400g baby spinach
250g ricotta cheese
200g Greek yogurt
30g grated Parmesan cheese
2 garlic cloves, crushed
zest of 2 lemons
10 fresh basil leaves, shredded
¼ tsp ground nutmeg
1 x 700g jar of tomato passata
fine sea salt and freshly ground
   black pepper

For the breadcrumb topping:
70g fresh breadcrumbs
70g grated Parmesan cheese
1 tsp chopped fresh thyme
1 tbsp butter, melted

Vegan Cashew Fusilli
in a Roasted Red Pepper Sauce

Serves 4 to 6

This veggie-packed pasta dinner is completely vegan —
and completely delicious!

METHOD

Start by soaking the cashews overnight in a bowl of cold
water, then drain and set aside.

Preheat the oven to 200°C.

Put the peppers on a baking tray and drizzle with
1 tablespoon of the oil. Roast in the preheated oven for 20
to 30 minutes, until the skins have blackened and charred.

Once the peppers are roasted, transfer them to a bowl,
cover it tightly with cling film and allow to sit for 15 minutes
to steam. When they are cool enough to handle, you should
be able to peel off the skins easily.

Meanwhile, cook the fusilli in a large pot of boiling salted
water for 8 to 10 minutes or according to the packet
instructions, until al dente. Drain.

Using a high-powered blender (a NutriBullet works well)
or a food processor, blitz the peppers with the soaked and
drained cashews, the remaining 4 tablespoons of olive oil
and the basil, lemon juice, nutritional yeast, smoked paprika
and a pinch of salt and pepper to form a smooth sauce.

Toss the cooked fusilli and the sauce together until all the
pasta is coated.

To serve, divide between warmed pasta bowls and sprinkle
with a little more nutritional yeast to finish.

100g raw cashews, soaked
   overnight
3 red peppers, halved
5 tbsp olive oil
400g egg-free fusilli
1 bunch of fresh basil
1 tbsp lemon juice
2 tbsp nutritional yeast, plus
   extra to serve
$\frac{1}{2}$ tsp smoked paprika
fine sea salt and freshly ground
   black pepper

PIZZA NIGHT

When it comes to making great pizza, it's all
about going back to basics. We've taken our
time perfecting our pizza dough recipe and
have put together some of our favourite topping
combinations so that you and yours can get together
and enjoy everyone's favourite – pizza night.

The beauty is
in the *basics*.

Pizza Basics

BASIC PIZZA DOUGH

Add the yeast to the lukewarm water and give it a stir, then leave it for 10 minutes, until it's foamy.

Put the flour and salt in the bowl of a stand mixer fitted with a dough hook. Add the activated yeast and the water, then mix on a medium speed for about 10 minutes, until it has come together into a smooth, elastic dough – you may need to add an extra splash of water to help it come together. Or if you're doing this by hand, mix everything together into a rough dough, then tip out onto a lightly floured countertop and knead for 12 to 15 minutes, until smooth.

Lightly oil the inside of two large bowls so that the dough won't stick to it. Divide the dough in half and shape each one into a neat ball. Place the dough in the bowls, cover tightly with cling film and allow to prove in a warm place for at least 90 minutes, until doubled in size.

Remove the cling film and knock the air out of the dough by making a fist and pushing it into the centre. When it has deflated, simply fold the edges of the dough into the centre and tuck it into a ball shape. Toss the dough in a little semolina, put each ball on a separate plate, cover tightly in cling film and store in the fridge until needed. You can make the dough up to two days ahead – in fact, the longer you leave it to rest in the fridge, the better the flavour will be and the easier the dough will be to work with, though it's also fine to use it straightaway.

Makes 2 medium pizzas or 1 extra-large

1 x 7g sachet of fast action dried yeast
175ml lukewarm water (about 45°C), plus extra if needed
300g '00' or strong white flour
1 tsp fine sea salt
olive oil, for greasing
semolina, for dusting

TOMATO AND HERB PIZZA SAUCE

Put the tomatoes, garlic and oregano in a saucepan and simmer on a medium heat for 8 to 10 minutes, until slightly reduced. Break down the tomatoes as they cook by crushing them lightly with a wooden spoon. Stir in the fresh basil.

You can use a hand-held blender to blitz it into a smooth sauce, but if you prefer a chunky sauce, then leave it as it is. Season to taste with salt and pepper.

Makes 250ml

1 x 400g tin of San Marzano tomatoes or whole plum tomatoes
1 garlic clove, crushed
1 tbsp chopped fresh oregano or 1 tsp dried
1 tbsp chopped fresh basil
fine sea salt and freshly ground black pepper

ARRABBIATA PIZZA SAUCE

It's the addition of chilli flakes that makes this arrabbiata, which translates as 'angry'. This sauce works just as well served with penne pasta with a little Pecorino grated on top as it does on a pizza.

Heat the oil in a saucepan on a medium heat. Add the onion and cook for 5 minutes, then add the garlic and chilli flakes and cook for 2 minutes more, stirring. Add the tomatoes and bay leaf and simmer for 8 to 10 minutes, until slightly reduced. Break down the tomatoes as they cook by crushing them lightly with a wooden spoon. Stir in the fresh basil. You can use a hand-held blender to blitz it into a smooth sauce (including the bay leaf or you can take it out before blending), but if you prefer a chunky sauce, then leave it as it is. Season to taste with salt and pepper.

MARGHERITA PIZZA

Preheat the oven to 240°C (or as hot as it will go) or fire up your pizza oven. Cover the ball of pizza dough with a light dusting of semolina to prevent the dough from sticking to the surface, then roll out into a 26cm circle. Spread the pizza sauce in a thin, even layer over the base, leaving 2cm to 3cm clear around the edge to form a crust, then scatter over the mozzarella. Cook in the preheated oven for anywhere from 10 to 15 minutes, depending on your oven, or 2 to 3 minutes in a pizza oven, until the base is cooked and golden and the cheese is melted and bubbling. Remove from the oven and scatter over the fresh basil leaves to serve.

CHEAT PIZZA

If you don't have time to make your own dough, a store-bought focaccia will do the trick if you're in a hurry (or you can try the focaccia recipe on page 68 if you fancy a change from the usual pizza dough base). Perfect for rustling up a quick dinner, simply dollop on some pizza sauce, add grated mozzarella and your favourite toppings. After 15 or 20 minutes in a hot oven, you'll have a deliciously simple pizza to slice up, share and enjoy.

Makes 250ml

2 tbsp olive oil
1 medium onion, chopped
3 garlic cloves, finely
   chopped
2 tsp chilli flakes
1 x 400g tin of San
   Marzano tomatoes or
   whole plum tomatoes
1 bay leaf
10 fresh basil leaves, torn
fine sea salt and freshly
   ground black pepper

Makes 1 pizza

1 ball of pizza dough
   (page 161)
semolina, for dusting
100ml tomato and herb
   pizza sauce (page 161)
60g Toonsbridge fior di
   latte mozzarella, torn
10 to 12 fresh basil leaves

Italian Sausage & Fennel Bianca

Makes 1 pizza

This pizza is definitely on the decadent side with the cream sauce and rich sausage. The fennel seeds add a pop of flavour too.

METHOD

Preheat the oven to 240°C (or as hot as it will go) or fire up your pizza oven.

Pour the cream into a small saucepan over a medium heat. Bring up to a simmer and cook until reduced by one-quarter – this should take 3 or 4 minutes.

Meanwhile, toast the fennel seeds in a hot dry frying pan over a medium-high heat for 2 or 3 minutes, until fragrant. Tip out onto a plate and set aside.

Cover the ball of pizza dough with a light dusting of semolina to prevent the dough from sticking to the surface, then roll out into a 26cm circle.

Spread the reduced cream in a thin, even layer over the base, leaving 2cm to 3cm clear around the edge to form a crust. Squeeze the sausage out of its skins and roll into small balls. Scatter the sausage and the rest of the ingredients evenly over the pizza.

Cook in the preheated oven for anywhere from 10 to 15 minutes, depending on your oven, or 2 to 3 minutes in a pizza oven, until the base is cooked and golden and the cheese is melted and bubbling.

100ml cream
½ tsp fennel seeds
1 ball of pizza dough (page 161)
semolina, for dusting
100g Italian sausage
60g fresh buffalo mozzarella, torn
30g fennel bulb, thinly sliced
¼ red onion, thinly sliced
2 tbsp grated Parmesan cheese
2 tsp finely chopped fresh oregano

Smoked Scamorza
with 'Nduja & Spicy Honey

Makes 1 pizza

Trust us when we say the honey works like magic on this pizza.

METHOD

The day before, put the honey and sliced chilli in a small saucepan and heat gently, then remove the pan from the heat, cover and allow to infuse for 24 hours. Alternatively, if you want an instant spicy honey, finely chop the chilli, add it to the heated honey and you can use it straightaway.

Preheat the oven to 240°C (or as hot as it will go) or fire up your pizza oven.

Cover the ball of pizza dough with a light dusting of semolina to prevent the dough from sticking to the surface, then roll out into a 26cm circle.

Spread the pizza sauce in a thin, even layer over the base, leaving 2cm to 3cm clear around the edge to form a crust, then scatter the three cheeses evenly over the sauce.

Using a teaspoon, dot the 'nduja around the pizza, then scatter over the garlic slices.

Cook in the preheated oven for anywhere from 10 to 15 minutes, depending on your oven, or 2 to 3 minutes in a pizza oven, until the base is cooked and golden and the cheese is melted and bubbling.

Remove from the oven and drizzle with the spicy honey.

4 tbsp honey
¼ fresh red chilli, deseeded and thinly sliced into rings
1 ball of pizza dough (page 161)
semolina, for dusting
100ml tomato and herb pizza sauce (page 161)
60g fresh buffalo mozzarella, torn
50g smoked scamorza cheese, thinly sliced
1 tbsp grated Parmesan cheese
50g 'nduja
1 garlic clove, thinly sliced

The G.O.A.T.

Makes 1 pizza

We may be biased, but we think Irish goat cheese is simply the best. Try it, you won't be disappointed!

METHOD

Preheat the oven to 240°C (or as hot as it will go) or fire up your pizza oven.

Cover the ball of pizza dough with a light dusting of semolina to prevent the dough from sticking to the surface, then roll out into a 26cm circle.

Spread the pizza sauce in a thin, even layer over the base, leaving 2cm to 3cm clear around the edge to form a crust.

Scatter the goat cheese, olives, mushrooms and red onion marmalade evenly over the pizza.

Cook in the preheated oven for anywhere from 10 to 15 minutes, depending on your oven, or 2 to 3 minutes in a pizza oven, until the base is cooked and golden and the cheese is melted and bubbling.

Remove from the oven and scatter over the toasted pine nuts and rocket to serve. If you're feeling extra indulgent, add a little more goat cheese.

1 ball of pizza dough (page 161)
semolina, for dusting
100ml tomato and herb pizza
    sauce (page 161)
80g goat cheese, plus extra to
    serve if you like
60g Kalamata olives, pitted
40g sliced oyster mushrooms
40g shop-bought red onion
    marmalade
1 tbsp pine nuts, toasted
a small handful of rocket

West Cork

Makes 1 pizza

We've opted for some of West Cork's finest ingredients here, from Gubbeen chorizo and Macroom buffalo mozzarella to Coolea cheese, to create an exquisite Irish pizza.

METHOD

Preheat the oven to 240°C (or as hot as it will go) or fire up your pizza oven.

Cover the ball of pizza dough with a light dusting of semolina to prevent the dough from sticking to the surface, then roll out into a 26cm circle..

Spread the pizza sauce in a thin, even layer over the base, leaving 2cm to 3cm clear around the edge to form a crust, then scatter over the chorizo and mozzarella.

Cook in the preheated oven for anywhere from 10 to 15 minutes, depending on your oven, or 2 to 3 minutes in a pizza oven, until the base is cooked and golden and the cheese is melted and bubbling.

Remove from the oven and scatter over the Coolea shavings.

1 ball of pizza dough
  (page 161)
semolina, for dusting
100ml tomato and herb
  pizza sauce (page 161)
80g Gubbeen chorizo,
  sliced
60g Macroom buffalo
  mozzarella, torn
20g Coolea cheese shavings

Chilli Chorizo
with Spicy Coriander Lime Dressing

Makes 1 pizza

This pizza doesn't need the traditional tomato-based pizza sauce – the burst of flavour from the coriander lime dressing is a delicious twist.

METHOD

Preheat the oven to 240°C (or as hot as it will go) or fire up your pizza oven.

First make the dressing by putting all the ingredients in a blender or food processor and blitzing until smooth, then season to taste with salt and pepper.

Cover the ball of pizza dough with a light dusting of semolina to prevent the dough from sticking to the surface, then roll out into a 26cm circle.

Evenly distribute the chorizo over the base, then scatter over the mozzarella, feta, Parmesan and the red and green chilli.

Cook in the preheated oven for anywhere from 10 to 15 minutes, depending on your oven, or 2 to 3 minutes in a pizza oven, until the base is cooked and golden and the cheese is melted and bubbling.

Remove from the oven and drizzle generously with the coriander lime dressing, then scatter over the chopped fresh coriander.

1 ball of pizza dough
  (page 161)
semolina, for dusting
20g sliced chorizo
60g fresh buffalo mozzarella,
  torn
50g feta cheese, crumbled
2 tbsp grated Parmesan cheese
½ fresh red chilli, deseeded
  and thinly sliced into rings
½ fresh green chilli, deseeded
  and thinly sliced into rings
1 tsp chopped fresh coriander

For the coriander lime dressing:
65g Greek yogurt
40g fresh coriander
3 garlic cloves, chopped
zest and juice of 2 limes
1 tsp finely chopped jalapeño
  pepper
fine sea salt and freshly ground
  black pepper

Chorizo, Roast Squash & Sage

Makes 1 pizza

Smoky chorizo meets sweet roasted squash to create a little magic in this scrumptious pizza.

METHOD

Preheat the oven to 180°C.

Put the butternut squash on a baking tray, drizzle with oil and season with salt and pepper. Roast in the preheated oven for 10 to 12 minutes, until almost soft.

Increase the oven temperature to 240°C (or as hot as it will go) or fire up your pizza oven.

To make the balsamic glaze, put the vinegar and brown sugar in a small saucepan. Bring up to a rolling simmer for 8 to 10 minutes, until it has reduced to a thick consistency that coats the back of a spoon. Set aside.

Cover the ball of pizza dough with a light dusting of semolina to prevent the dough from sticking to the surface, then roll out into a 26cm circle.

Spread the pizza sauce in a thin, even layer over the base, leaving 2cm to 3cm clear around the edge to form a crust, then evenly distribute the roasted squash, chorizo, sage, mozzarella and Parmesan over the sauce.

Cook in the preheated oven for anywhere from 10 to 15 minutes, depending on your oven, or 2 to 3 minutes in a pizza oven, until the base is cooked and golden and the cheese is melted and bubbling.

Remove from the oven and drizzle with the balsamic glaze.

150g butternut squash, peeled and cut into 2cm pieces
a drizzle of rapeseed oil, for roasting
1 ball of pizza dough (page 161)
semolina flour, for dusting
100ml tomato and herb pizza sauce (page 161)
80g dry-cured chorizo, diced
4 fresh sage leaves, roughly torn
60g fresh buffalo mozzarella, torn
2 tbsp grated Parmesan cheese
fine sea salt and freshly ground black pepper

For the balsamic glaze:
100ml balsamic vinegar
50g light brown sugar

Mushroom
with a Vegan Cauliflower Béchamel

Makes 1 pizza

The cauliflower béchamel sauce on this vegan pizza gives it a creamy richness, while the onion marmalade and mushrooms provide real depth of flavour.

METHOD

Preheat the oven to 180°C.

Put the sliced mushrooms on a baking tray. Drizzle with the oil, scatter over the rosemary and thyme and toss to coat, then roast in the preheated oven for 8 to 10 minutes, until softened. Allow to cool.

When the mushrooms come out of the oven, increase the temperature to 240°C (or as hot as it will go) or fire up your pizza oven.

Meanwhile, to make the cauliflower béchamel, put the cauliflower rice and almond milk in a small saucepan and cook on a medium-high heat for 5 or 6 minutes, until the cauliflower is nice and soft and the liquid has reduced by half.

Heat the oil in a separate small frying pan over a low heat. Add the onion, thyme and nutmeg along with a good pinch of salt and pepper and cook for a few minutes, until softened. Add to the almond milk and cooked cauliflower, then blitz with a hand-held blender (or in a food processor) until completely smooth. Set aside.

Cover the ball of pizza dough with a light dusting of semolina to prevent the dough from sticking to the surface, then roll out into a 26cm circle.

Spread the béchamel sauce in a thin, even layer over the base, leaving 2cm to 3cm clear around the edge to form a crust. Top with the mushrooms and dot the onion marmalade around the pizza with a teaspoon.

Cook in the preheated oven for anywhere from 10 to 15 minutes, depending on your oven, or 2 to 3 minutes in a pizza oven, until the base is cooked and the béchamel sauce is bubbling.

90g portobello mushrooms, sliced
30g shiitake mushrooms, sliced
3 tbsp rapeseed oil
1 tsp finely chopped fresh rosemary
1 tsp finely chopped fresh thyme
1 ball of pizza dough (page 161)
semolina, for dusting
2 tbsp shop-bought onion marmalade

For the cauliflower béchamel:
60g cauliflower, grated into 'rice'
160ml almond milk
1 tbsp rapeseed oil
40g diced onion
½ tsp fresh thyme
a pinch of ground nutmeg
fine sea salt and freshly ground black pepper

FISH SUPPERS

When it comes to fish, the fresher, the better. In
Ireland we are fortunate to be able to enjoy an
abundance of fresh fish thanks to our lucky little
spot in the wild Atlantic.

From our *lucky little* spot in the wild Atlantic.

FROM THE SEA

Here in Ireland, we're spoiled for choice when it comes to fish. There is an abundance of flat fish, from turbot to plaice and sole, perfect for baking and grilling. Other delicious native fish include monkfish, John Dory and haddock, to name just a few. Shellfish such as lobster, crawfish, crab, mussels and oysters also thrive on our Atlantic shores.

Ireland has a long-standing tradition of smoking and preserving fish, from the prized Atlantic salmon to soused herrings and mackerel. If you fancy trying your hand at catching your own, there's nothing more delicious than freshly caught mackerel sizzling on the barbecue.

We've put together a few of our favourite recipes from the sea, from old favourites like fishcakes to delicious tray-baked fish for the family and impressive garlicky gambas.

Avoca Fish Cakes

Makes 4

Our fish cakes are a tried-and-tested, time-honoured favourite at our deli counters. What's our secret? We roast our seafood mix instead of poaching or steaming it to enhance the flavour and to help the (characteristically generous!) fish cakes keep their shape.

METHOD

Preheat the oven to 180°C.

To make the tartare sauce, simply mix all the ingredients together, season to taste and set aside in the fridge until needed.

Roast the seafood mix on a baking tray in the preheated oven for 6 minutes. Set aside and allow to cool. Turn off the oven at this stage.

Put the mashed potatoes in a large bowl with the spring onions, fresh herbs, lemon juice, mustard, chilli flakes and a generous pinch of salt and pepper. Mix thoroughly.

Add the roasted seafood mix, stirring them in gently so that you have big lumps throughout the fish cakes. This will make all the difference to the texture and appearance of your fish cakes.

Shape the mix into four large cakes. Place on a plate, cover with cling film and chill in the fridge for at least 30 minutes (but 1 hour is better if you have the time).

Preheat the oven to 180°C again. Line a baking tray with non-stick baking paper.

To assemble your crumbing station, you'll need three separate wide, shallow bowls. Put the flour in the first bowl and season it with some salt and pepper, then put the beaten eggs in the second bowl and the breadcrumbs in the third bowl. Have a plate at the end of your assembly line to put the crumbed fish cakes on.

Continues ...

500g seafood chowder mix
400g cooked mashed potatoes
2 tbsp finely chopped
    spring onions
1 tsp finely chopped fresh dill
1 tsp finely chopped fresh flat-
    leaf parsley
1 tsp lemon juice
¼ tsp wholegrain mustard
⅛ tsp chilli flakes
50g plain flour
2 eggs, beaten
100g panko breadcrumbs
4 tbsp rapeseed oil
fine sea salt and freshly ground
    black pepper

For the tartare sauce:
300g mayonnaise
juice of ½ lemon
1 large gherkin, finely chopped
1 shallot, finely diced
1 dessertspoon chopped capers
1 tbsp chopped fresh dill
1 tbsp chopped fresh flat-leaf
    parsley
1 tsp Dijon mustard

To serve:
baby gem wedge salad with
    smoked almond and caper
    gremolata (page 80)
lemon wedges

METHOD CONTINUED

Dip the cakes in the flour first, gently brushing or shaking off any excess, then dip in the beaten eggs to coat, again shaking off any excess, before adding to the breadcrumbs. Make sure each cake is completely and evenly covered in the flour, beaten egg and breadcrumbs as you move along. Finally, place the crumbed cakes on the plate, ready for cooking.

Heat the oil in a large non-stick frying pan over a medium heat. Add the fish cakes (working in batches if necessary so that you don't overcrowd the pan) and fry for a few minutes on each side, until golden brown. Transfer to the lined baking tray and cook in the oven for 8 to 10 minutes, until completely heated through.

Serve with the baby gem wedge salad, the tartare sauce on the side and lemon wedges for squeezing over.

Soy & Ginger Glazed Salmon

Serves 4

We love this sweet and sticky glaze on salmon, but it works well on any white fish too. Unbelievably quick and simple, this tasty dish is a perfect midweek meal served with fluffy basmati rice and our rainbow sesame slaw.

METHOD

Blitz all the marinade ingredients together and set one-quarter aside in the fridge for basting.

Put the rest of the marinade in a baking dish. Add the salmon fillets and coat both sides with the marinade. Cover with cling film and marinate in the fridge for 6 to 8 hours or overnight.

Take the salmon out of the fridge 30 minutes before you bake it to bring the fish back to room temperature, which will help it to cook evenly.

Preheat the oven to 180°C. Line a baking tray with foil.

Transfer the salmon to the lined tray and cook in the preheated oven for 7 minutes, then baste the salmon with the marinade you set aside earlier. Return to the oven and cook for another 5 to 7 minutes, until firm to the touch. Once the salmon has finished cooking, baste it once more with the remaining glaze. Serve with basmati rice and the crunchy rainbow sesame slaw on the side.

4 x 160g organic salmon fillets

For the marinade:
20g peeled and grated fresh
   ginger
1 garlic clove, crushed
40g shop-bought plum sauce
2 tbsp sweet soy sauce
4 tsp sesame oil
4 tsp water
2 tsp soy sauce

To serve:
boiled basmati rice
crunchy rainbow sesame slaw
   (page 98)

Seared Garlic
& Chilli Gambas
with Toasted Sourdough

Serves 4

This speedy dish not only tastes incredible, but it looks great too. Whether you serve it as an impressive brunch dish, as part of a tapas spread or as the main event, it's a real crowd pleaser.

METHOD

Toast the sourdough on a hot griddle pan over a high heat until nice char marks form. Rub one side of the toast with the cut side of the garlic clove and brush with a little extra virgin olive oil. Set aside and keep warm.

Heat the rapeseed oil in a large frying pan over a medium heat. Add the gambas and cook on each side for 90 seconds. Once the colour of the shells changes to a reddish-orange colour, add the garlic, chillies and some salt and pepper and cook briefly, just until the oil takes on a red tinge.

Increase the heat to high, then add the white wine and lemon juice. Let it bubble up and cook for 4 minutes, then add the butter. The sauce should thicken and develop a velvety shine.

Right at the end, add the chopped parsley and give it a quick toss.

Transfer to serving plates, with the warm grilled sourdough on the side for mopping up all the sauce. Serve with a few lemon wedges for squeezing over.

3 tbsp rapeseed oil
500g gambas, shells and heads
  still on
5 garlic cloves, thinly sliced
2 fresh red chillies, deseeded and
  thinly sliced
200ml white wine
juice of 2 lemons, plus extra
  wedges to serve
100g unsalted butter, diced
10g fresh flat-leaf parsley,
  roughly chopped
fine sea salt and freshly ground
  black pepper

For the toasted sourdough:
1 loaf of sourdough bread, sliced
1 garlic clove, cut in half
extra virgin olive oil, for
  brushing

When writing your shopping list...

SHOPPING

You may need to order the gambas in advance from your fishmonger.

Baked Haddock
with Bombay Potatoes

Serves 4

This meaty North Atlantic fish combines with the Indian-spiced potatoes to create a hearty fish supper perfect for sharing and serving family-style.

METHOD

Cook the potatoes in boiling salted water for 10 to 12 minutes, until they are nearly cooked but still a little firm in the centre. Drain and set aside.

Heat 1 tablespoon of the oil in a large non-stick frying pan over a medium heat. Add the shallot and cook for 30 seconds, then add the curry powder, tomato purée and a generous pinch of salt. Cook for 1 minute, stirring constantly.

Add the parboiled potatoes to the pan and cook for a further 6 to 8 minutes, until the potatoes are fully cooked and have crisped up a bit but are still holding their shape and not falling apart. Remove the pan from the heat.

Heat the remaining tablespoon of oil in a separate non-stick frying pan over a medium heat. Season the haddock with salt and pepper, then place it in the hot pan, skin side up, and cook for 2 minutes. Don't move the fish around, just allow it to sit there for the full 2 minutes.

Add the butter to the pan, then carefully turn over the fillets and cook for a further 2 minutes. As the butter melts and begins to foam, baste the fish with it for 1 or 2 minutes more. Every fillet of fish is different, so if a fillet is a little thicker than the others, it may need another minute or two.

Put the pan with the potatoes back on a medium heat. Add the chard and a squeeze of lemon juice and cook for 1 minute, just until it's heated through.

Transfer the fish to four serving plates. Add the peas to the pan you cooked the fish in and cook for 1 minute in the buttery pan juices.

To serve, place the Bombay potatoes and peas onto your serving plate and top with the haddock.

8 medium Rooster potatoes, peeled and cut into 2cm dice
2 tbsp rapeseed oil
1 shallot, finely diced
2 tbsp curry powder
1 tbsp tomato purée
4 haddock fillets, skin on
1 tbsp butter
200g rainbow chard (or baby spinach), chopped
1 tsp lemon juice
200g fresh or frozen peas
fine sea salt and freshly ground black pepper

Pan-fried Mackerel
with Golden Beetroot & Blood Orange Salsa

Serves 4

This zingy salsa does a wonderful job of cutting through the rich mackerel. One of our top tips for mackerel? Ask your fishmonger to 'V cut' it for you to save you some tricky work with the bones.

METHOD

Preheat the oven to 180°C.

Start by putting the beetroot on a large sheet of tin foil with the garlic clove and drizzling over a tablespoon of oil. Wrap up the tin foil into a parcel, making sure it's tightly sealed. Place the parcel on a baking tray and roast in the oven for 1 hour 20 minutes, until the beetroot are completely cooked through – a knife should slide through them easily. When they're done, open the parcel, being careful of the escaping steam, and allow to cool for 40 minutes. (Discard the garlic clove, it's done its job now as a flavour infuser.) When they're cool enough to handle, peel the beetroot and cut into small dice.

Cut the orange segments in half and put them in a large bowl along with the diced beetroot and preserved lemons, dill, lemon juice and some salt and pepper to taste. Toss to combine.

Heat a large non-stick frying pan over a high heat. Once the pan is smoking hot, season the mackerel with salt and pepper and add the tablespoon of oil, then add the mackerel to the hot pan, skin side down. Turn the heat down to medium and cook for 3 to 4 minutes, depending on the size of the fillets – they should be almost completely cooked through. Flip the fillets over and take the pan off the heat. Allow the fish to finish cooking in the residual heat of the pan for 1 or 2 minutes.

Serve the mackerel with a hearty portion of the golden beetroot and blood orange salsa. This would also be delicious served with some potato salad.

4 mackerel fillets, 'V cut'
   and skin on
1 tbsp rapeseed oil

For the salsa:
2 medium golden beetroot
1 garlic clove, left whole and
   unpeeled
1 tbsp rapeseed oil
1 blood orange, peeled and
   segmented
30g preserved lemons, finely
   chopped
1 tbsp finely chopped fresh dill
1 tbsp lemon juice
fine sea salt and freshly ground
   black pepper

To serve:
potato salad

When writing your shopping list...

SHOPPING

If you can't get golden beetroot or blood oranges, you can always use the regular versions of both.

Roast Cod

with Tomato Salsa & Green Beans

Serves 4

Fresh and flavoursome, this cod dish is delicious and
satisfying.

METHOD

To make the salsa, simply mix all the ingredients and season
well with salt and pepper. Set aside to let the flavours marry
together at room temperature.

Blanch the green beans in a pan of boiling salted water for
2 minutes, then drain. Set aside.

Heat the rapeseed oil in a large non-stick frying pan over
a medium-high heat. Add the hake fillets, skin side down,
and cook for about 5 minutes, until the skin is golden. Add
the butter, flip the fish over, season with salt and pepper
and cook for 2 to 3 minutes more, basting with the melted
butter, until fully cooked. Remove the fish from the pan and
transfer to a plate lined with kitchen paper.

Add the edamame and green beans to the same pan,
raise the heat to high and toss for 1 to 2 minutes, until the
edamame are cooked through.

Serve the hake on a bed of the beans with some salsa on the
side and a spoonful of tapenade on top of each fillet.

120g green beans, halved
2 tbsp rapeseed oil
4 x 160g cod fillets, skin on
30g butter
120g edamame beans, thawed
tapenade (page 233)

For the salsa:
3 ripe heirloom tomatoes
  (various colours if possible),
  deseeded and diced
2 ripe plum tomatoes, deseeded
  and diced
$\frac{1}{2}$ small red onion, finely diced
juice of 1 lime
2 tbsp extra virgin olive oil
2 tbsp chopped capers
2 tbsp chopped fresh flat-leaf
  parsley
fine sea salt and freshly ground
  black pepper

FEASTS & GATHERINGS

Good food brings people together. There's no
better feeling than gathering your nearest and
dearest around the dinner table, dishing up a
delicious meal prepared with love and watching
them tuck in and enjoy. Whether you're hosting a
dinner party, a family reunion or throwing a party,
our recipes promise clean plates and happy guests.

Good food brings
people *together.*

THE AVOCA BUTCHER

At our butchers, you'll find a selection of Irish, artisan, organic and free-range meat. We have a passionate food team who scour the country from top to bottom – from Wicklow to Kildare and Meath to Mayo, we're proud to work closely with some of Ireland's finest farmers. Dedicated to Irish provenance and sourcing quality ingredients, we discuss everything with our suppliers, from welfare and quality of feed to the importance of livestock roaming freely over fields, orchards and mountain pastures.

Whether you're planning on cooking a rack of pork for your Sunday roast, steaks on the barbecue or beef shin for a hearty slow-braised stew, our knowledgeable butchers are always happy to share their expert advice on how best to prepare and cook meat at home. Not only skilled butchers but fantastic home cooks themselves, our butchers love to chat about everything from the best cuts for specific recipes to recommendations on rubs, sauces and marinades. They're always available to share their expertise to help you get the most out of your meats – and they might even throw in a few bones or offcuts to take home for the dog!

SETTING THE SCENE

Nothing brings people together like good food. Whether you love to host large get-togethers or prefer to keep it casual, we believe every gathering can, and should, be memorable. A beautifully decorated table is a wonderful way to make your gatherings feel extra special. A good rule of thumb is to set your table in keeping with your own personal style and décor – do what feels right for you.

Gatherings should be relaxed and fun, so even if you're the host you can still sit back and enjoy yourself, the good food and the great company. Rather than overly fussy dishes, meticulous place settings or traditional dinner party formalities, you can always opt for sharing platters, help-yourself dinners and natural tablescapes.

Serving family-style from giant bowls or sharing platters is a simple option when feeding a crowd. Pop a handful of cutlery in a jug, set out a stack of napkins and let everyone help themselves. Celebrate the perfectly imperfect when it comes to hosting and with the right people around your table and delicious, simple food made from great ingredients, you can't go wrong.

Create a feeling of laid-back warmth with a mishmash of glassware, hand-me-downs and heirlooms, which are perfect for adding a personal touch. As long as everyone around the table has enough space to relax and enjoy a meal prepared with love and care, you're on to a winner.

Confit Duck Legs
with All the Trimmings

Serves 4

If you want to wow your dinner guests with something that wouldn't be out of place on the menu of a French bistro, this is the recipe for you. Pair with a glass of red wine and twinkling candlelight.

METHOD

To confit the duck, salt the duck legs the day before, using ½ tablespoon of sea salt per duck leg. Rub into the skin and meat thoroughly and leave overnight. The next day wash and pat the duck legs dry. Place them in a deep ovenproof dish and cover with the duck fat. They should be completely immersed. Cook in a preheated oven at 160°C for 2 hours, until the meat is tender. If you are stuck for time you can pick up good quality ready-prepared duck confit at your local food market and cook according to the packet instructions.

Preheat the oven to 160°C. Line a baking tray with non-stick baking paper.

Start by making the parsnip crisps. Place the parsnip ribbons on the lined tray, then drizzle over the honey, season lightly with salt and pepper and toss to coat. Cook in the preheated oven for 20 minutes, until crisp and golden. Remove to a wire rack and scrape them up off the paper with a fish slice so they don't stick as they cool on the tray.

Increase the oven temperature to 180°C.

Meanwhile, to make the Parmesan potato galette, brush a 30cm loose-bottomed quiche tin with some of the melted butter. Layer the potatoes in the tin in a fan shape, starting from the outer edge and working your way to the centre.

Continues ...

For the confit duck legs:
8 large duck legs
1kg duck fat
4 tbsp sea salt
or 8 ready-prepared
  confit duck legs

For the parsnip crisps:
1 parsnip, peeled into long strips
1 tbsp honey

For the Parmesan potato galette:
2 tbsp melted butter
6 medium Rooster potatoes,
  peeled and thinly sliced
100g Parmesan cheese, grated

For the vegetables:
4 to 6 large carrots, peeled, halved
  and cut into thirds
½ large turnip, peeled and cubed
  into large bite-sized pieces
a knob of butter

For the red wine jus:
1 tbsp rapeseed oil
1 large shallot, diced
300ml red wine
600ml beef stock
1 sprig of fresh thyme
20g butter, diced
fine sea salt and freshly ground
  black pepper

METHOD CONTINUED

Each slice should slightly overlap the previous slice. Brush each layer with the melted butter and sprinkle over the grated Parmesan, making sure you keep some Parmesan for the final scattering later on. When complete, press a sheet of greaseproof paper directly on top of the galette and then cover the tin tightly with foil. Cook in the oven alongside the duck for 35 to 40 minutes, until a knife can slide through the potatoes without any resistance.

Remove from the oven and take off the foil, then put a heavy saucepan on top of the greaseproof paper to compress the galette. Press it down gently, but not so much that you squash the potatoes. Remove the paper, top with the remaining Parmesan and put it back in the oven to cook for 10 to 15 minutes, until golden.

To make the red wine jus, heat the oil in a small saucepan over a medium heat. Add the shallot and cook for only 30 to 45 seconds, then add the thyme and red wine, increase the heat to high and boil for 6 to 7 minutes, until the wine has reduced by half. Add the beef stock and boil for another 15 minutes, until reduced by half. Strain the jus through a fine mesh sieve, then return to the pan and whisk in the butter until it emulsifies and the jus is glossy.

When the duck is almost finished cooking, cook the carrots and turnip in a saucepan of boiling salted water for 8 to 10 minutes, until cooked through and tender. Toss with a knob of butter and season lightly with salt and pepper.

Serve two duck legs per person alongside a slice of the Parmesan potato galette and the carrots and turnips. Spoon over the red wine jus, then finish with the parsnip crisps and a good dollop of red onion marmalade.

To serve:
4 tbsp shop-bought red onion marmalade

Our chefs let us in on a little secret...

CHEF'S TIP

Remember to keep your duck fat, it makes the best roast potatoes.

Roast Turbot
with Salsa Verde & Sautéed Greens

Serves 4 to 6

Turbot is a real treat. A large saltwater fish known for its firm, white flesh and delicate flavour, it's taken up a notch with this zingy salsa verde. If you can't find turbot, halibut will work a treat.

METHOD

Preheat the oven to 180°C.

To make the salsa verde, mix together the capers, gherkins and shallots with 4 tablespoons of the oil and the herbs, adding a little more oil if you like. Add the lemon juice to taste – it shouldn't need any extra seasoning due to the salty capers and gherkins. Set aside to let the flavours marry together.

Score the skin of the turbot all around the edges to make it easier to lift off the skin after cooking. Put the lemon slices over the base of a roasting tray, then put the turbot on top. Scatter the diced butter over the turbot and season with salt and pepper. Roast in the preheated oven for 25 to 30 minutes, until fully cooked. The turbot is ready when the flesh is creamy white and lifts from the centre bone easily.

Towards the end of the turbot's cooking time, heat the rapeseed oil in a large frying pan over a medium heat. Add the cavolo nero and cook, stirring, for 2 minutes, then add the spinach and cook for 1 minute more. Remove the pan from the heat, season with salt and pepper and allow the greens to wilt gently in the residual heat of the pan.

Blanch the green beans in a pan of boiling salted water for 2 minutes, then drain.

Place the turbot on a large serving dish, peel off the skin and spoon the salsa verde over the fish. Serve with the sautéed greens, blanched green beans and buttery steamed baby potatoes.

1 x 1.2kg to 1.5kg whole turbot
  (see the intro)
2 lemons, sliced
50g butter, diced

For the sautéed greens:
4 tbsp rapeseed oil
200g cavolo nero, stems
  removed
200g baby spinach
fine sea salt and freshly ground
  black pepper

For the green beans:
200g fine green beans

For the salsa verde:
50g capers, finely chopped
50g gherkins, finely chopped
50g shallots, finely chopped
4 to 6 tbsp extra virgin olive oil
2 tbsp chopped fresh flat-leaf
  parsley
2 tbsp chopped fresh tarragon
juice of 1 lemon

To serve:
steamed baby potatoes

When writing your shopping list...

SHOPPING

Pre-order the whole fish a few days ahead of time from your fishmonger. It's worth asking them if they can gut it for you too.

Avoca Glazed Ham

Serves 10 to 12

Our famous glazed ham is perfect for feasts and gatherings.
A much-loved classic since the very beginning of Avoca, this
sweet, tender ham is everyone's favourite and you'll soon see why.
Enjoy the leftovers the next day between thickly sliced bread
spread with lashings of Irish butter.

A gammon is typically large, ranging from 5kg to 8kg, so before
you start, make sure you have a pot, tray and oven large enough
to cook this fantastic cut of meat. Ask your butcher in advance
for gammon on the bone, as they won't always have it in stock.
It's best to plan a week ahead when ordering. Gammons aren't
as salty as they once were, so soaking them overnight is often no
longer necessary, but check with your butcher to be certain.

METHOD

Place the gammon in a large pot of water along with the onions,
cloves and bay leaves, making sure the water covers the gammon.
Bring to the boil, then reduce to a simmer. The gammon needs
to cook for 45 to 50 minutes per kilo. We typically use a gammon
that weighs about 7kg, so that takes between 5½ to 6 hours
to cook. You will have to top up the water every hour or so to
ensure the meat is always kept covered. Use hot water when
topping up the pot, as cold water will reduce the temperature of
your pot and therefore increase the cooking time. Skim off the
impurities that gather on the surface periodically.

Once cooked, allow the ham to cool in the water for 2 to 3
hours. Drain the water and carefully transfer the ham to a
roasting tin. Remove the top layer of skin from the ham, leaving
about 1.5cm of fat.

Preheat the oven to 190°C.

To make the glaze, mix together the sugar, mustard and
some salt and pepper to form a thick paste and coat the meat
thoroughly. Roast in the preheated oven for 25 to 30 minutes,
until nicely caramelised on top.

Allow the ham to rest for 20 minutes before carving.

1 x 6kg to 7kg bone-in
   gammon
2 large onions, peeled
   and halved
10g cloves
6 bay leaves

For the glaze:
500g Demerara sugar
150g Dijon mustard
fine sea salt and freshly
   ground black pepper

Slow-cooked Chipotle Beef Tacos

Serves 6

Beautifully slow-cooked, this chipotle beef is guaranteed to melt in your mouth. Serve with guacamole for a complete taco night get-together.

METHOD

Mix all the dry rub ingredients together. Put the beef in a large baking dish or tray and coat it all over with the dry rub. Cover with cling film or foil and leave in the fridge overnight.

The next day, put the rubbed brisket in a slow cooker with the cola, chillies and garlic. Cover with a lid and cook on the low setting for 8 hours or for 4 hours on high.

To make the paste, put the onion, garlic, chillies, chipotle chilli paste, liquid smoke (if using) and half the coriander in a food processor and blitz for a few minutes to form a smooth paste.

Heat the rapeseed oil in a frying pan over a medium-low heat. Add the paste and cook, stirring occasionally, for 6 to 8 minutes, until most of the liquid has evaporated.

Preheat the oven to 180°C.

Transfer the beef from the slow cooker to a roasting tray and spread the paste evenly over the top. Carefully ladle some of the cooking liquid from the slow cooker around the beef in the roasting tray. Cook in the preheated oven, uncovered, for 30 minutes, basting the beef every 10 minutes. Remove from the oven and allow to rest for 30 minutes, then transfer to a serving bowl. The beef should be so meltingly tender that you can shred it with two forks. Drizzle over some of the cooking juices and garnish with the remaining chopped fresh coriander.

Continues ...

1.5kg beef brisket
1 litre cola
2 fresh red chillies, cut in half
4 garlic cloves, unpeeled and
    smashed

For the dry rub:
50g light brown sugar
1 tbsp smoked paprika
1 tbsp ground coriander
1 tbsp onion powder
1 tbsp ground black pepper
2 tsp fine sea salt
1 tsp garlic powder

For the paste:
2 red onions, roughly chopped
4 garlic cloves, roughly chopped
2 fresh red chillies, deseeded and
    roughly chopped
50g chipotle chilli paste
3 tbsp liquid smoke (optional)
10g fresh coriander
5 tbsp rapeseed oil

For the coriander rice:
350g basmati rice
750ml water
50g fresh coriander, roughly
    chopped
juice of ½ lime
¼ tsp fine sea salt

METHOD CONTINUED

While the beef is resting, make the coriander rice. Put the rice and water in a large heavy-based pot and bring to the boil, then cover with a tight-fitting lid and reduce to a low simmer. When all the water has been absorbed, remove the pan from the heat and allow to rest for 5 minutes, then fluff up the rice gently with a fork. Add the chopped coriander, lime juice and salt and fold it through the rice using a rubber spatula.

Just before serving, make the guacamole so that the avocado doesn't turn brown. Scoop the avocados out of their skins with a spoon into a pestle and mortar and add the remaining ingredients. Bash everything together for 2 or 3 minutes, until fully incorporated but ideally with some chunks of avocado throughout for added texture. Season to taste with salt and pepper.

To serve, bring the bowl of shredded chipotle beef to the table with plates of warm corn tortillas and bowls of the guacamole and let everyone assemble their own tacos, with coriander rice on the side.

For the guacamole:
3 ripe avocados, halved and stoned
1 large ripe tomato, diced
1 fresh red chilli, deseeded and finely chopped
juice of 1 lime
3 tbsp finely chopped red onion
3 tbsp chopped fresh coriander
fine sea salt and freshly ground black pepper

Spatchcock Chicken

Serves 6

Ideally, use an organic free-range chicken for this dish. The Avoca butchers will not only supply this, but they will also spatchcock the chicken for you. To spatchcock simply means removing the backbone and spreading the chicken out flat, therefore reducing the amount of time it takes to cook. You can cook this in the oven, but it's also a great one for the barbecue.

METHOD

Whisk together the oil, fresh herbs and spices. Score the chicken on the thickest part of the drumsticks to help ensure it cooks evenly. Coat the chicken in the spices, rubbing into the scored drumsticks. Allow to sit, covered, overnight in the fridge.

Preheat the oven to 170°C.

Put the onions and peppers on a baking tray and sit the chicken on top, skin side up. Season with salt and pepper, then roast in the preheated oven for 60 to 70 minutes, until the chicken reaches an internal temperature of 75°C on a digital meat thermometer.

Alternatively, this is a great dish to cook on the barbecue. Simply place the chicken on the grill rack, skin side up, and cook for 60 to 70 minutes over an indirect heat before flipping it over and placing it directly above the hot coals to crisp up the skin.

Allow to rest for 10 to 15 minutes before carving and serving with the baby gem wedge salad.

4 tbsp rapeseed oil
2 sprigs of fresh rosemary, needles stripped
1 tbsp finely chopped fresh oregano
1 tbsp smoked paprika
1 tbsp cayenne pepper
1 whole organic, free-range chicken, spatchcocked
2 medium onions, halved
1 red pepper, quartered
1 yellow pepper, quartered
fine sea salt and freshly ground black pepper

To serve:
baby gem wedge salad with smoked almond and caper gremolata (page 80)

When writing your shopping list...

SHOPPING

If you are hosting a crowd you can prepare more than one chicken!

Beef Bourguignon
with Roast Baby Potatoes

Serves 4

At Avoca, we love the classics when it comes to cooking and there is nothing more classic than a beef bourguignon. Try to use a good quality burgundy if you can. Ask your butcher if they can acquire beef shin. It's not regularly available in supermarkets or butcher counters, but if you can get it, it will bring this dish to the next level.

METHOD

Preheat the oven to 150°C.

Toss the beef in the flour and season generously with salt and pepper.

Heat 1 tablespoon of the olive oil in a large frying pan over a medium heat. Working in batches so that you don't crowd the pan, add the beef and cook until it's nicely browned all over, then transfer to a large plate with a slotted spoon. You may need to add a little more oil in between the batches if the pan is too dry.

Deglaze the pan with the red wine and allow it to come to the boil, stirring to scrape up any browned bits from the bottom of the pan, which are full of flavour. Set the pan aside.

Heat the remaining olive oil in a large heavy-based casserole dish over a medium heat. Add the onion and cook for 5 to 8 minutes, until softened and translucent. Add the garlic and bacon lardons and cook for a few minutes, until the garlic is fragrant and the bacon has picked up some colour.

Add the browned beef along with the deglazed pan juices and the bay leaf. Add half the thyme and rosemary sprigs, then add the tinned tomatoes and tomato purée. Cook for 1 or 2 minutes, then stir in the beef stock, making sure the

Continues ...

1kg diced beef (chump, shin or topside, with a good marbling of fat)
3 tbsp plain flour
4 to 5 tbsp olive oil
250ml red wine (Burgundy is traditional)
1 large onion, finely diced
2 garlic cloves, crushed
150g bacon lardons
1 bay leaf
3 sprigs of fresh thyme
2 sprigs of fresh rosemary
1 x 400g tin of chopped tomatoes
1 tsp tomato purée
500ml beef stock
150g baby button mushrooms
100g pearl onions
fine sea salt and freshly ground black pepper

For the roast baby potatoes:
600g baby potatoes
2 tbsp olive oil
1 tsp chopped fresh rosemary

To serve:
tossed green salad

METHOD CONTINUED

stock covers the beef. Bring to the boil, then cover with a tight-fitting lid and transfer to the preheated oven to cook for 2½ hours.

Discard the thyme sprigs, then add the mushrooms and pearl onions. Chop the remaining thyme and rosemary, and add to the casserole too. Return to the oven, uncovered, and cook for a further 30 minutes, until the beef is tender. Taste to correct the seasoning, then keep warm over a low heat on the hob while you make the roast potatoes.

Increase the oven temperature to 180°C.

Toss the potatoes in the oil and rosemary until they are coated. Place on a baking tray and roast in the oven for 20 to 25 minutes, until fork tender.

To serve, ladle the beef bourguignon into warm shallow bowls with the roast baby potatoes and a tossed green salad on the side.

Aubergine Parmigiana

Serves 6

This is a showstopper of a dish. We use a combination of Parmesan and Pecorino for extra flavour.

METHOD

Preheat the oven to 180°C.

Put a ridged chargrill pan over a medium-high heat to get it good and hot and brush both sides of the aubergine slices lightly with oil. Working in batches so that you don't overcrowd the pan, add a single layer of aubergine slices to the hot pan. Cook for a few minutes on each side, until nice char marks have formed and the aubergines have softened. Set aside on a plate while you cook the rest.

To assemble, cover the base of a large baking dish with a single layer of chargrilled aubergine slices – you should aim to use half the slices. Sprinkle with some porcini dust (if using), then scatter over one-third of the torn mozzarella, one-third of the grated Parmesan and Pecorino and half the basil leaves, then ladle over half the tomato and herb sauce. Repeat the layers, then dot the top with the remaining mozzarella and grated cheese.

Cook in the preheated oven for 25 to 30 minutes, until the cheese is bubbling and the aubergines and sauce are piping hot. Allow to stand for at least 15 minutes before serving straight to the table with a large bowl of crisp green salad and warm focaccia.

4 aubergines, sliced into thick circles
olive oil, for brushing
2 tbsp porcini dust (optional)
2 balls of buffalo mozzarella, torn
80g Parmesan
80g Pecorino
20 fresh basil leaves
2 or 3 batches of tomato and herb pizza sauce (page 161)
fine sea salt and freshly ground black pepper

To serve:
lightly dressed crisp green salad
focaccia (page 68)

Baked Field Mushrooms

with Wicklow Brie & Onion Marmalade

Serves 4

This vegetarian dish is so simple to rustle up and looks mouth-wateringly beautiful served in your favourite roasting tin. A delicious starter for a crowd, a side dish or veggie main, we recommend using Wicklow Brie, one of our favourite Irish farmhouse cheeses.

METHOD

Preheat the oven to 200°C.

To make the balsamic syrup, simply put the vinegar and maple syrup in a small saucepan over a medium heat and simmer until it has reduced by two-thirds and coats the back of a spoon. This should take 10 to 12 minutes. Set aside.

Put the mushrooms on a baking tray, underside facing up, and add the stalks too. Drizzle with oil and season well with salt and pepper. Cook in the preheated oven for 8 minutes, then remove from the oven and place a slice of Brie on top of each mushroom. Return to the oven and cook for about 5 minutes more, until the mushrooms are cooked and the Brie has melted.

To serve, chop the mushroom stalks and scatter them around the edges of the mushrooms, on top of the cheese. Place a heaped tablespoon of the onion marmalade in the centre and drizzle with the balsamic syrup. Serve with a lightly dressed watercress salad on the side.

8 large field or portobello mushrooms, stalks removed and reserved
rapeseed oil, for drizzling
240g Wicklow Brie cheese, cut into 8 x 30g slices

For the balsamic syrup:
200ml balsamic vinegar
4 tbsp maple syrup

To serve:
shop-bought onion marmalade
lightly dressed watercress salad

SHARING PLATTERS & BOARDS

For grazing, sharing, tasting and nibbling while pouring,
sipping, chatting and laughing, you can mix and match these
platters and boards whether it's for a party of two or ten. The
beauty of our food markets is that you can pick up an array
of delicious nibbles and bites, pop them on your favourite
sharing board and you're good to go. From Irish farmhouse
cheeses and juicy olives to tapenade, hummus and baba
ghanoush and from biscuits, crackers and freshly baked bread
to Irish smoked salmon, it couldn't be easier to rustle up a
stellar sharing platter for your favourite people.

For grazing, *sharing*, tasting & nibbling.

Antipasti

An assorted antipasti platter is always a winner, perfect for nibbling, sharing and enjoying with friends. Some Italian essentials such as prosciutto di Parma, bresaola, porchetta and speck are always a wonderful addition to any antipasti platter, although there are Irish charcuterie options too. Some slices of toasted ciabatta, olive oil and balsamic vinegar would make this platter complete.

TAPENADE

Rinse the olives in a colander under cold running water, then drain and put in a blender along with the olive oil, garlic, capers, anchovies, lemon juice and thyme. Blitz until smooth.

Serve as part of your antipasti board. Spoon any leftovers into a jar and store in the fridge for up to a week.

Serves 4

340g Kalamata olives, pitted
100ml good-quality extra virgin olive oil
2 garlic cloves, finely chopped
3 tbsp capers
2 tbsp chopped tinned anchovies
2 tbsp lemon juice
1 tbsp chopped fresh thyme

TUSCAN CANNELLINI BEAN & ROSEMARY DIP

Heat the olive oil in a small frying pan over a medium heat. Add the garlic and cook for about 3 minutes, until golden. Remove the pan from heat and stir in the rosemary and chilli flakes, then allow to cool slightly.

Put the beans, a generous pinch of salt and all but 1 teaspoon of the rosemary oil in a food processor or blender and blitz until smooth.

Pour the dip into a serving bowl and drizzle with the reserved rosemary oil. Serve as part of your antipasti board.

Serves 4

5 tbsp extra virgin olive oil
3 garlic cloves, finely chopped
1 sprig of fresh rosemary, finely chopped
¼ tsp chilli flakes
1 x 400g tin of cannellini beans, drained and rinsed
fine sea salt and freshly ground black pepper

CAPONATA

Heat the oil in a medium-sized saucepan over a medium heat. Add the aubergine and a pinch of salt and cook for 10 to 12 minutes, until softened. Use a slotted spoon to transfer the aubergines to a plate and set aside.

Add the shallots and celery to the oil left behind in the pan. Reduce the heat to low and cook for 6 to 8 minutes, until the shallots are translucent. Add the tomatoes and cook for 5 or 6 minutes, until they begin to break down.

Add the olives, raisins, vinegar, capers, sugar and 1 tablespoon of the pine nuts. Cook on a low heat for 20 minutes, then allow to cool.

Spoon the caponata into a serving bowl and top with the remaining pine nuts and the torn basil. Serve at room temperature as part of your antipasti board.

Serves 4

5 tbsp extra virgin olive oil
2 aubergines, cut into 2cm dice
3 shallots, chopped
2 celery stalks, sliced
3 plum tomatoes, diced
30g green olives, pitted and
  halved
4 tbsp golden raisins
3 tbsp red wine vinegar
1 tbsp capers
1 tbsp caster sugar
2 tbsp pine nuts, toasted
15 fresh basil leaves, torn
fine sea salt and freshly ground
  black pepper

Mezze Board

When it comes to a mouth-watering mezze platter, we recommend the trio of baba ghanoush, falafel and courgette fritters served with plenty of flatbread (page 70), shop-bought hummus and a selection of crackers or breadsticks.

BABA GHANOUSH

Char the whole aubergines on a gas flame for 8 to 10 minutes, turning every 30 seconds. When they're cool enough to handle, peel off the skin and remove the stalk. Or if you don't have a gas hob, you can cut the aubergines in half, place them on a baking tray cut side up and roast in an oven preheated to 190°C for 25 to 30 minutes, then when they're cool enough to handle, scoop out the flesh with a spoon, discarding the skins.

Put the charred or roasted aubergines in a blender or food processor with the remaining ingredients and blend for 1 or 2 minutes, until smooth. Season to taste with salt and pepper, then blend briefly again.

Transfer the baba ghanoush to a serving bowl and top with a drizzle of extra virgin olive oil and a pinch of paprika. Serve with warm flatbread.

Serves 6

2 small aubergines
1 garlic clove, chopped
3 tbsp extra virgin olive oil, plus extra to garnish
1 tbsp lemon juice
½ tbsp tahini
¼ tsp paprika, plus extra to garnish
fine sea salt and freshly ground black pepper

To serve:
warm flatbread (page 70)

When writing your shopping list...

SHOPPING

Choose aubergines that are firm and small, as they tend to have fewer seeds.

CRUNCHY SESAME FALAFEL WITH TZATZIKI

If using dried chickpeas, soak them in a large bowl of cold water overnight. The next day, drain and put them in a pot of fresh cold water, making sure the water is 10cm above the chickpeas. Bring to the boil, then reduce the heat and simmer for 45 minutes to 1 hour, until tender. Drain and allow to cool.

Meanwhile, to make the tzatziki, squeeze out any excess water from the grated cucumber. Mix with the yogurt, garlic, lemon zest and juice and the fresh mint, then season to taste with salt and pepper. Cover the bowl with cling film and set aside in the fridge until needed.

Toast the cumin and coriander seeds in a hot dry frying pan over a high heat for 1 or 2 minutes, just until fragrant, then grind in a spice or coffee grinder for 30 seconds.

Put the cooled drained chickpeas in a large mixing bowl with the ground cumin and coriander seeds along with the red onion, garlic, chilli, fresh herbs, sesame seeds, cayenne and a generous seasoning of salt and pepper. Mash everything together using a potato masher (or blend everything together in a food processor if you prefer). Taste and adjust the seasoning.

Add the beaten egg and mix it in thoroughly with your hands. If the mix is a little too wet and likely to break up when you fry it, add 1 or 2 tablespoons of plain flour to bring it all together. Shape the mix into balls about 50g each.

Heat the oil in a deep-fryer to 180°C.

Working in batches, deep-fry the falafel for 8 to 10 minutes, until golden brown and firm. Tip out onto a wire rack set over a baking tray lined with kitchen paper to absorb any excess oil.

Serve hot or cold with the tzatziki on the mezze board.

Serves 6

250g dried chickpeas or
  2 x 400g tins of chickpeas,
  drained and rinsed
1 tsp cumin seeds
1 tsp coriander seeds
1 small red onion, finely diced
1 garlic clove, crushed
½ fresh red chilli, finely chopped
2 tbsp finely chopped fresh flat-
  leaf parsley
2 tbsp finely chopped fresh
  coriander
1 tbsp finely chopped fresh mint
2 tbsp sesame seeds
¼ tsp cayenne pepper
1 large egg, beaten
sunflower oil, for deep-frying
fine sea salt and freshly ground
  black pepper

For the tzatziki:
1 medium cucumber, deseeded
  and grated
200g Greek yogurt
1 garlic clove, grated
1 tbsp lemon zest
1 tbsp lemon juice
1 tsp finely chopped fresh mint
fine sea salt and freshly ground
  black pepper

Our chefs let us in on a little secret...

CHEF'S TIP

For the most authentic texture our chefs like to use dried chickpeas and soak them overnight before cooking.

COURGETTE FRITTERS

Put the grated courgettes and carrots into a clean tea towel and squeeze out as much moisture as you possibly can. This will help to keep them from breaking up while they cook.

Put the grated courgettes and carrots in a large bowl with the grated onion, spices and a generous pinch of salt and pepper. Give it a good mix and taste a little to see if it needs more salt or pepper. Stir in the flour and allow to sit for 1 minute before adding the beaten eggs, mixing thoroughly until well combined.

Heat the oil in a large frying pan over a medium-high heat. Working in batches so that you don't crowd the pan, add heaped tablespoons of the mixture to the pan and flatten immediately with the back of the spoon. Fry for 2 to 3 minutes on each side, until golden and crisp. Transfer to a plate lined with kitchen paper to absorb any excess oil while you cook the remaining fritters.

Serve as part of your mezze board.

Serves 6

3 medium courgettes, grated
2 medium carrots, peeled and
    grated
1 small onion, grated
1 tbsp ground coriander
2 tsp ground turmeric
2 tbsp plain flour
2 large eggs, beaten
100ml sunflower oil
fine sea salt and freshly ground
    black pepper

Bagna Càuda

It's such a simple, joyful thing to put together a dipping board for sharing. Just a few delicious ingredients, some fresh local vegetables, your favourite bread or crackers and you're practically there! The hero dip here is bagna càuda, a traditional Italian dip from the Piedmont region made with a generous helping of anchovies and garlic. A beautiful assortment of bread and fresh veg is perfect for this board and looks wonderful too. Think artichoke hearts, green beans, roast cauliflower, organic carrots, steamed baby potatoes … the list is endless.

METHOD

Preheat the oven to 160°C.

Cut the carrots and celery into finger-length batons.

Peel the garlic and cut each clove in half. Remove any green sprouts that may be inside the cloves, as they can add a bitterness that you don't want.

Put the milk in a small saucepan over a medium heat. Add the peeled, halved garlic cloves and simmer gently for 15 to 20 minutes, until most of the milk has evaporated and the garlic is softened.

Pour the oil into a separate small saucepan over a low heat. Add the anchovies and cook for 6 to 8 minutes, until they soften and even melt a little. Add the butter and continue to cook for 2 to 3 minutes, until melted. Remove the pan from the heat, add the garlic and allow to cool for 10 minutes. Using a hand-held blender, blitz the garlic and anchovy oil until smooth.

It's best to serve this dish warm, so if you can, pour the bagna càuda into a small flameproof casserole and keep it warm over a small flame, like a tealight (or if you happen to have a fojòt – a small ceramic or porcelain dish from Piedmont made especially for serving bagna càuda – even better).

Cut the bread into similar-sized sticks as the vegetables. Place on a baking tray and brush with a little of the olive oil, then toast in the preheated oven for 10 minutes, until crisp.

Serve with the warm toasted bread and the carrot and celery batons for dipping.

Serves 6

2 large carrots, peeled
4 celery stalks
100ml extra virgin olive oil
2 heads of garlic
300ml milk
12 tinned anchovy fillets
90g butter
a selection of your favourite
   vegetables
1 loaf of crusty sourdough
   bread

Ultimate Cheeseboard

Several of our Avoca locations have wonderful cheese and charcuterie counters. There are no hard and fast rules when it comes to cheeseboards, as it's important to choose what you like, but it's always a good idea to go for balance. Including a cow, goat and sheep cheese as well as different textures is a great place to start. Once you've chosen a selection of your favourite cheeses, dish up these delicious accompaniments along with some charcuterie, fresh fruit and plenty of crackers and enjoy.

PEAR AND SHALLOT CHUTNEY

Put the brown sugar, vinegar and brandy in a small saucepan. Bring to the boil, then reduce the heat and simmer for 3 to 4 minutes, until the brown sugar has dissolved.

Add the rest of the ingredients and simmer for 25 to 30 minutes, until thickened and sticky. Allow to cool, then serve with your favourite crackers and cheese as part of the ultimate cheeseboard.

This will keep for up to two months in an airtight container in the fridge.

Serves 6

120g light brown sugar

130ml apple cider vinegar

2 tbsp brandy

4 ripe pears, cut into 1cm dice

3 shallots, finely chopped

80g sultanas

$\frac{1}{2}$ tsp ground cinnamon

$\frac{1}{2}$ tsp ground ginger

$\frac{1}{4}$ tsp ground nutmeg

One of our foodie favourites...

TASTE TIP

Add some nibbed almonds if you prefer something a little nuttier.

FIG AND ALMOND COMPOTE

Place the figs, brown sugar and diced apple in a small saucepan over a medium heat and cook for 8 to 10 minutes, until the apples have started to soften and the sugar has dissolved. Add the brandy and cook for a further 2 to 3 minutes, until the alcohol evaporates.

Remove the pan from the heat and stir in the almonds and apple juice, then allow to cool.

Serve with your favourite crackers and cheese as part of the ultimate cheeseboard. This will keep in an airtight container in the fridge for up to a week.

Makes 1 x 500g jar

250g dried figs, diced
90g light brown sugar
1 Granny Smith apple, peeled, cored and diced
2 tbsp brandy
90g whole blanched almonds
4 tbsp apple juice

ROASTED RED PEPPER CHUTNEY

Preheat the oven to 210°C.

Put the peppers on a baking tray, then roast in the preheated oven for about 20 minutes, until their skins are blackened and charred.

Transfer the roasted peppers to a bowl, cover it tightly with cling film and allow to sit for 10 to 15 minutes to steam. When they are cool enough to handle you should be able to peel off the skins easily, then deseed and chop the roasted peppers.

Meanwhile, heat the oil in a small saucepan over a medium-high heat. Add the red onion, garlic and chilli and cook for 3 or 4 minutes, until the onion has started to soften. Add the sun-dried tomatoes and roasted red peppers along with the mustard. Reduce the heat to low and cook for 8 to 10 minutes, until the flavours have married together, then transfer to the blender or food processor and pulse for a few seconds – it shouldn't be completely smooth.

Serve as a zingy addition to the ultimate cheeseboard. This will keep in an airtight jar in the fridge for up to a week.

Serves 4 to 6

4 red peppers
2 tbsp rapeseed oil
1 medium red onion, chopped
2 garlic cloves, chopped
1 fresh red chilli, deseeded and finely chopped
90g sun-dried tomatoes in oil
1 tbsp Kasundi mustard
fine sea salt and freshly ground black pepper

When writing your shopping list...

SHOPPING

Well worth adding to your shopping list, Kasundi mustard is a delicious and spicy store cupboard item.

Seafood Platter

Serves 6

Is there a better showstopper when feeding a crowd than a spectacular seafood platter? The oysters Rockefeller add an extra-special touch.

METHOD

Preheat the oven to 220°C. Pour a thick layer of rock salt or coarse sea salt over a baking tray for the oysters to sit on later.

For the oysters Rockefeller, melt the butter in a large frying pan over a low heat. Add the shallot and a pinch of salt and cook for about 3 minutes, until softened, then add the breadcrumbs and fresh herbs and mix well. Remove the pan from the heat and mix in the grated Pecorino cheese and some salt and pepper.

Spoon the breadcrumbs onto the oysters in the half shells. Place on the bed of salt on the baking tray and cook in the preheated oven for 6 to 7 minutes, until golden brown. Set aside.

You'll need two large frying pans on the go now: one for the gambas and Dublin Bay prawns and one for the scallops. (The crab claws are already cooked, so you'll simply heat them through at the end.)

Heat 2 tablespoons of rapeseed oil in the first pan over a medium-high heat. Add the gambas, garlic and paprika and cook for 2 minutes before adding the Dublin Bay prawns, chilli, white wine and butter and seasoning lightly with salt and pepper. Cook for 4 to 6 minutes, tossing constantly, until all the prawns and gambas are pink and completely cooked through. Remove the pan from the heat, toss with the parsley and dill and set aside.

Continues ...

For the oysters Rockefeller:
rock salt or coarse sea salt
100g butter
1 shallot, finely diced
100g fresh breadcrumbs
1 sprig of fresh thyme, leaves stripped
1 tsp finely chopped fresh flat-leaf parsley
1 tsp finely chopped dill
60g grated Pecorino Romano cheese
12 oysters, shucked, detached and put back in the half shell
fine sea salt and freshly ground black pepper

For the gambas and Dublin Bay prawns:
2 tbsp rapeseed oil
6 gambas, shells and heads still on
2 garlic cloves, finely chopped
1 tsp sweet paprika
6 Dublin Bay prawns
1 fresh red chilli, deseeded and finely chopped
50ml white wine
50g butter
2 tbsp finely chopped fresh flat-leaf parsley
2 tbsp finely chopped fresh dill

METHOD CONTINUED

Pat the scallops dry on kitchen paper, then season both sides with a pinch of salt. Heat the oil in a separate large heavy-based frying pan or sauté pan over a high heat. Once the pan is smoking hot, add the scallops, leaving room in between them to prevent them from steaming. Cook for 1 to 1½ minutes, just until they are nicely browned. Flip the scallops and cook for 1 minute more, until the second side is browned. Transfer the scallops to a plate lined with kitchen paper.

Wipe the pan clean with some kitchen paper and put it back over a medium-high heat. Add the butter, smashed garlic and thyme and cook until the butter starts to foam.

Remove the garlic and thyme, then add the crab claws to the pan and heat through for 2 to 3 minutes, tossing in the butter. Finish with a squeeze of lemon.

Arrange all the cooked seafood on a large platter and serve with wedges of lemon, some freshly chopped dill and slices of our buttered famous brown bread.

For the scallops:
300g scallops, corals removed
2 tbsp rapeseed oil
90g butter
2 garlic cloves, lightly smashed
½ tsp finely chopped fresh thyme (or lemon thyme if it's growing in your garden)

For the crab claws:
12 cooked crab claws
a squeeze of lemon juice

To serve:
2 lemons, cut into wedges
chopped fresh dill
Avoca's famous brown bread (page 66)

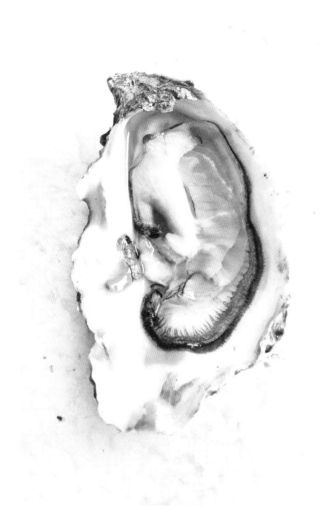

CAKES & DESSERTS

There's nothing quite like a home-baked cake or your
favourite homemade dessert and no better feeling
than serving it up to a table of eager, smiling faces.
Even just the aroma of a cake baking in the oven is
enough to set hearts aflutter.

We don't mean to blow our own trumpet, but we're
famous for our cakes – and the very generous helpings of
them we dish out in our cafés and food markets! At Avoca,
we're honoured that our cakes and desserts have
become a little part of the tradition of so many
birthdays, celebrations, parties and gatherings.
With this selection of cakes and desserts, now you can
recreate your favourites at home.

Nothing makes
an *occasion* quite
like cake.

Cherry Berry Chocolate Roulade

Serves 8

Perfect as a festive dessert, this chocolate roulade makes a delicious treat all year round too. The fact that it's quick and simple to prepare is (literally) the cherry on top!

METHOD

Whip the cream until soft peaks form. Put about 50g into a piping bag for the top later, then put both the piping bag and the bowl in the fridge for now.

Preheat the oven to 160°C. Line a 23cm x 33cm Swiss roll tin with non-stick baking paper.

To make the roulade base, whisk the egg yolks, sugar and vanilla until pale, then sift in the cocoa powder and whisk again until combined.

In a separate spotlessly clean, dry bowl, whisk the egg whites until soft peaks form. Add one-quarter of the egg whites to the chocolate mixture to loosen it, then fold in the remaining whites until the mixture is an even colour with no white spots.

Pour the mixture onto the lined tray and spread it out evenly with a palette knife to cover the base. Bake in the preheated oven for 16 to 18 minutes, until firm.

Take a large sheet of non-stick baking paper (a little larger than the roulade base) and sprinkle with a little cocoa powder, then flip the warm sponge onto the paper so that the baking paper that's underneath the base is now facing up. Peel the baking paper away from the warm base.

Continues ...

For the roulade base:
6 eggs, separated
150g caster sugar
1 tsp vanilla extract
55g cocoa powder, plus
  extra for dusting

For the filling:
200ml cream
50g glacé cherries,
  chopped

To decorate:
30g fresh blackberries
30g Amarena cherries in
  syrup, drained
a few whole glacé cherries

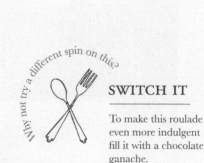

Why not try a different spin on this?

SWITCH IT

To make this roulade even more indulgent fill it with a chocolate ganache.

METHOD CONTINUED

Roll up the sponge tightly and carefully in the paper and allow to cool completely. This method will help prevent the sponge from splitting when rolling it again later.

When the sponge is cool, unroll it carefully but leave the paper under it. Spoon the whipped cream onto the sponge base and use a palette knife to spread it out thinly and evenly. Sprinkle the chopped cherries on top.

Using the paper, slowly ease the sponge over the filling to begin rolling it. Roll it carefully and try to keep it tight. Once rolled, place in the fridge for 30 minutes. Slice an inch off each end to tidy it up.

To decorate, neatly place the blackberries and cherries in a line running down the centre of the top. Cut into slices to serve.

Clementine Curd Naked Cake

Serves 10

A real showstopper, this is a wonderful celebration cake.
Make this for a loved one's birthday to really push the
boat out.

METHOD

Preheat the oven to 170°C. Grease and line 3 x 23cm
springform cake tins (or use just one tin, divide the batter
into thirds and bake each layer one at a time).

Beat the eggs, sugar and zest with an electric hand mixer
or in the bowl of a stand mixer fitted with the paddle
attachment on a high speed for 1 or 2 minutes, until
pale and thick. Add the olive oil in a slow, steady stream
while still beating on a high speed. This should take 3
to 4 minutes. Add the yogurt and continue to beat for 3
minutes, until fully incorporated, then beat in the vanilla
extract and orange oil.

In a separate bowl, mix together the flour, baking powder
and salt. Add the flour mixture to the sugar and egg
mixture in three increments, beating each time until
combined.

Divide the batter evenly between the three greased
and lined tins. Bake in the preheated oven for 22 to 24
minutes, until a skewer inserted into the centre comes out
clean. Allow to cool in the tins for 5 minutes, then remove
from the tins and allow to cool completely on a wire rack.

To make the curd, put the eggs, yolks, butter, sugar,
zest and juice in a heatproof bowl set over a pan of
simmering water, making sure the water doesn't touch

Continues ...

For the cakes:
9 eggs
450g caster sugar
zest of 3 clementines
350ml olive oil
360ml natural yogurt
2½ tsp vanilla extract
2 tsp orange oil
565g plain flour
4 tsp baking powder
a pinch of fine sea salt

For the clementine curd:
4 eggs
6 egg yolks
160g unsalted butter, diced
160g caster sugar
5 clementines (zest of 2 and
    300ml juice)

For the filling:
500ml cream

Why not try a different spin on this?

SWITCH IT

Try this recipe with
limes instead of
clementines.

METHOD CONTINUED

the bottom of the bowl. Whisk continuously over the heat for about 10 minutes, until the curd thickens. When it hits 70°C to 75°C on a candy thermometer, scrape the curd into a clean bowl. Press a sheet of cling film directly on top of the curd so that a skin doesn't form and place in the fridge to cool down.

Whip the cream just slightly beyond soft peaks and set aside in the fridge too.

To assemble, you want the cake layers to be nice and flat, so using a sharp carving knife, cut the tops from the three cakes to make them more even, but they don't have to be perfect, as they will be covered up with the whipped cream and curd.

Place the first cake on a cake stand or serving plate with the freshly cut side facing upwards. Add one-quarter of the cream and spread it out to the edges with a palette knife. Drizzle one-quarter of the curd over the whipped cream.

Place the next cake on top of the first layer with the freshly cut side facing down and repeat the layers of whipped cream and curd. The final cake layer is also placed with the freshly cut side facing down. Add the rest of the whipped cream to the top so that it completely covers it, then add the rest of the curd to the top of the cream. Use a clean palette knife to carefully smooth the curd on top.

Using the same palette knife, smooth the outer edges of the cake. A little of the cream should cover the edges, but it should remain mostly exposed.

Chill in the fridge for 30 minutes before cutting into slices to serve.

Triple Ginger Cake

Serves 8 to 10

An oldie but a goodie, we've taken our time perfecting our ginger cake recipe. Try baking it in a Bundt tin for a traditional version at Christmastime.

METHOD

Preheat the oven to 160°C. Grease and line a 23cm cake tin.

Put the flour, sugar, ground ginger and mixed spice in a large bowl (or the bowl of a stand mixer fitted with the paddle attachment) and mix well.

Put the treacle and golden syrup in a medium-sized saucepan, then pour in the just-boiled water from the kettle. Add the baking soda and stir to combine – the baking soda will fizz up. Stir in the oil.

Make a well in the centre of the dry ingredients and beat in the hot treacle mixture in three increments, adding an egg in between the first two additions and beating until fully incorporated.

Pour the batter into the greased and lined tin and bake in the preheated oven for 30 to 35 minutes, until a skewer inserted into the centre of the cake comes out clean.

Meanwhile, to make the ginger syrup, put the sugar, ginger and water in a small saucepan and bring to the boil, then reduce the heat to medium-low and simmer for 25 minutes, stirring occasionally. Remove the pan from the heat and keep warm.

When the cake is done, remove it from the tin, transfer to a plate and pour the warm ginger syrup all over it.

Sprinkle the chopped crystallised ginger all around the edges to decorate. Cut into slices and serve while still warm, with softly whipped cream or a scoop (or two!) of vanilla ice cream.

butter, for greasing
320g plain flour, sieved
175g caster sugar
2 tsp ground ginger
2 tsp mixed spice
80g treacle
80g golden syrup
240ml boiling water from
   the kettle
2 tsp baking soda
180ml sunflower oil
2 eggs

For the ginger syrup:
500g caster sugar
100g fresh ginger, peeled
   and cut into 4 pieces
500ml water

To decorate:
20g crystallised ginger,
   chopped

To serve:
softly whipped cream
   or vanilla ice cream

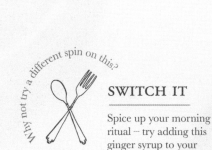

Why not try a different spin on this?

SWITCH IT

Spice up your morning ritual – try adding this ginger syrup to your morning cup of coffee.

Apple & Blackberry Crumble Cake

Serves 8 to 10

Somewhere between a crumble and a cake, this dessert is
the best of both worlds. Humble apples and blackberries
are the perfect autumn match, topped with a sweet
blackberry compote.

METHOD

Preheat the oven to 160°C. Grease and line a 23cm loose-
bottomed tart tin.

Make the crumble topping first. Put the flour and sugar in
a medium-sized bowl and mix together, then add the diced
butter and use your fingertips to rub it in until it resembles
breadcrumbs. Set aside.

Cream the butter and sugar together until pale and fluffy.
Add the eggs one at a time, waiting until each one is fully
incorporated before adding the next one.

Mix the flour and cinnamon together in a separate bowl,
then add to the egg mix and mix until just combined. Fold in
the apples and blackberries.

Scrape the batter into the prepared tin and smooth the top.
Scatter over the crumble topping and bake in the oven for 40
minutes, until golden and a skewer inserted into the centre
comes out clean.

Allow the cake to cool for 15 minutes in the tin, then remove
and place on a wire rack to cool completely.

While the cake bakes and cools, make the compote. Put the
blackberries, sugar and lemon juice in a small heavy-based
saucepan over a low heat. Cook until the sugar has dissolved,
then increase the heat to medium-high and simmer for 8 to
10 minutes, stirring often, until thickened slightly.

Cut the cooled cake into slices and serve with the warm
compote and softly whipped cream.

For the cake:
175g butter, at room temperature
175g caster sugar
3 eggs
350g self-raising flour
1 tsp ground cinnamon
400g apples, peeled, cored and grated
100g fresh blackberries, cut in half

For the crumble topping:
140g plain flour
50g caster sugar
85g butter, diced

For the blackberry compote:
250g fresh or frozen blackberries
50g caster sugar
1 tbsp lemon juice

To serve:
softly whipped cream

Espresso Crème Brûlée
with Amaretti Biscuits

Serves 4

One of our chefs loves all things coffee and created an excellent flavour balance with this dessert. The bitterness of the coffee paired with the sweetness of the caramelised top and the velvet texture of the crème brûlée, served with a beautifully simple amaretti biscuit, is a coffee lover's dream.

METHOD

Preheat the oven to 140°C.

To make the crème brûlée, beat the egg yolks and sugar together in a large heatproof bowl until pale, then add the espresso and vanilla extract and beat for 2 minutes.

Heat the cream in a pot until it has almost boiled – you will see bubbles at the edges when it's almost at the boiling point.

While whisking constantly, gradually add the hot cream to the sugar and egg mixture in small increments. Don't add the cream too fast or it may scramble the mixture.

Place a fine mesh sieve on top of a jug and pour this custard through the sieve to make sure it's perfectly smooth.

Pour the custard into four ramekins and set them in a roasting tin. Pour boiling water from the kettle into the roasting tin until it comes halfway up the sides of the ramekins. Transfer to the preheated oven and bake for 35 minutes. The custard should be set but should still jiggle slightly in the centre.

Remove the ramekins from the tray and allow to cool for 45 minutes before covering with cling film and placing in the fridge to chill for 6 hours or overnight.

To make the amaretti biscuits, preheat the oven to 170°C. Line a baking tray with non-stick baking paper.

Continues ...

6 egg yolks
80g caster sugar, plus extra
   for topping
1 tsp vanilla extract
500ml fresh cream
50ml espresso

For the amaretti biscuits:
1 egg white
95g ground almonds
90g caster sugar
2 tsp amaretto
¼ tsp vanilla extract

METHOD CONTINUED

Whisk the egg white in a medium-sized bowl until stiff peaks form, then fold in the ground almonds, sugar, amaretto and vanilla extract until it becomes a light-yellow paste.

Place a heaped teaspoon of the mixture onto the lined baking tray, making sure you keep the spoonfuls spaced 2cm to 3cm apart as they will expand while cooking.

Bake in the preheated oven for 15 minutes, until golden brown and set. Allow to cool on the tray for 5 minutes before transferring to a wire rack to cool completely.

Just before you serve, sprinkle a heaped teaspoon of caster sugar on top of each ramekin and caramelise the sugar with a kitchen blowtorch – use a circular motion to achieve the best result. If you don't have a kitchen blowtorch, preheat the grill to its hottest setting. Put the ramekins on a tray and place them under the grill until the sugar has fully caramelised, then return the ramekins to the fridge for 10 minutes.

Serve the crème brûlée with one or two amaretti biscuits on the side.

Chocolate Fudge Cake

Serves 10

Our chocolate fudge cake is famous and you'll soon taste why! Shamelessly decadent and gloriously chocolatey, it's best served gently warmed with a dollop of your favourite ice cream.

METHOD

Preheat the oven to 170°C. Grease and line the bases of 2 x 23cm springform cake tins.

Sift the flour, cocoa powder and baking soda into a large bowl, then stir in the caster sugar.

In a separate bowl, whisk together the eggs, milk, sunflower oil and golden syrup. Make a well in the dry ingredients and pour in the wet ingredients, then beat together until smooth.

Divide the batter evenly between the two greased tins and bake in the preheated oven for about 30 minutes, until risen and firm to the touch and a skewer inserted into the middle comes out clean. Allow to cool in the tins for 15 minutes before turning out and transferring to a wire rack to cool completely.

To make the icing, sift the icing sugar and cocoa powder together into a large bowl. Add the butter and beat for 8 minutes with a hand mixer on medium speed, until smooth. It may look really dry, but it will come together at about the 7 minute mark. Add a tablespoon of milk if needed to make the icing fluffy and spreadable.

To assemble, you want the cake layers to be nice and flat, so using a sharp carving knife, cut the tops from the cakes to make them more even but they don't have to be perfect, as they will be covered up with the icing.

Put the first cake on a cake stand or serving platter, cut side up. When icing the cake, have a jug of hot water nearby to dip your palette knife into. This will help to smooth the surface and spread the icing more easily. Spread a generous

Continues ...

For the cake:
butter, for greasing
360g self-raising flour
55g cocoa powder
2 tsp baking soda
300g caster sugar
6 eggs, beaten
300ml milk
300ml sunflower oil
130g golden syrup

For the icing:
400g icing sugar
100g cocoa powder
250g unsalted butter, at room
    temperature
1 tbsp milk (if needed)

For the chocolate shavings:
1 bar of good-quality chocolate

To serve:
your favourite ice cream

METHOD CONTINUED

layer of the icing over the top using a palette knife. Your knife should be sitting in a jug of hot water and wiped with a clean cloth before each use to help spread the icing smoothly.

Place the second cake on top of the first layer with the freshly cut side facing down. Spread the rest of the icing over the top and sides of the cake, again using the hot palette knife to achieve a smooth finish.

To make the chocolate shavings, place the chocolate bar flat side up and scrape the surface quite firmly with a small, sharp knife. Keeping the knife upright, pull it towards you to create the chocolate shavings.

To decorate, scatter the shavings over the edges of the cake. To serve, cut into slices and gently warm it in the microwave for 10 seconds before adding a scoop of your favourite ice cream alongside.

Seriously Rich Flourless Chocolate Orange Cake

Serves 8

This flourless cake certainly isn't lacking when it comes to decadence or deliciousness. If you'd like to skip the Cointreau, try a tablespoon of orange oil instead.

METHOD

Preheat the oven to 160°C. Butter and line a 23cm springform cake tin.

Put the butter and chocolate in a heatproof bowl set over a pan of simmering water, making sure the water doesn't touch the bottom of the bowl. Allow to melt, then stir to combine and set aside for 5 minutes to cool slightly.

Stir the ground almonds, egg yolks, orange zest and Cointreau or orange oil into the melted butter and chocolate.

In a spotlessly clean, dry bowl, whisk the egg whites until soft peaks form. Gradually add the sugar and continue to whisk until stiff peaks form.

Stir one-quarter of the egg whites into the chocolate mixture to loosen and lighten it. Add the rest of the egg whites and gently fold in until no white is visible and the batter is light and airy, then pour into the lined cake tin.

Bake in the preheated oven for 30 to 40 minutes, until well risen and just firm. Allow to cool completely in the tin on a wire rack (it will sink a bit as it cools) before removing from the tin.

Meanwhile, to make the buttercream, beat the butter, icing sugar and orange oil together on a low speed for about 5 minutes. At the start it may seem like it's too much icing sugar, but it will come together. Once it has come together into a smooth buttercream, add half the orange zest.

Top the cake with the buttercream, then scatter over the remaining zest to decorate.

100g butter, diced, plus extra for greasing
140g dark chocolate (at least 70% cocoa solids), chopped
140g ground almonds
6 eggs, separated
zest of 2 oranges
1 tbsp Cointreau or orange oil
85g caster sugar

For the buttercream:
1 x 227g block of unsalted butter, at room temperature
500g icing sugar
4 tsp orange oil
zest of 1 orange

Glossy Chocolate & Peanut Butter Pie

Serves 8 to 10

There are few more delicious pairings than chocolate and peanut butter. The glossy chocolate ganache topping gives this dessert a luxurious, lustrous finish.

METHOD

Preheat the oven to 180°C.

First make the crust. Melt the butter and golden syrup together in a small saucepan, then pour it over the crushed digestives and stir to combine. Press firmly and evenly into the base and up the sides of a 23cm loose-bottomed tart tin. Bake in the preheated oven for 10 minutes, then allow to cool on a wire rack.

To make the filling, beat the cream cheese, peanut butter and sugar together, then fold in the whipped cream. Spoon onto the biscuit base and smooth the top, then chill in the fridge while you make the topping.

To make the topping, put the sugar and cream in a medium-sized saucepan over a medium heat. As soon as it comes to the boil – and keep a close eye on it, as you don't want to scald the cream and also because it can quickly bubble up and over the sides of the saucepan – reduce the heat and simmer for about 5 minutes, until it has thickened slightly and turned a pale yellow colour. Remove from the heat and stir in the chocolate and butter until they have melted and the ganache is nice and smooth. Allow to cool slightly, then pour on top of the tart. Chill for 1 hour in the fridge, until the filling and topping have both set firm.

For the crust:
100g butter
2½ tbsp golden syrup
250g digestive biscuits,
   crushed into crumbs

For the filling:
250g full-fat cream cheese
170g chunky peanut butter
55g caster sugar
180ml cream, whipped

For the topping:
30g caster sugar
140ml cream
60g dark chocolate, finely
   chopped
30g butter, diced

CAKES & DESSERTS 275

Cinnamon & Apple Crumble Cheesecake

Serves 8 to 10

This baked cheesecake is a show-stopping centrepiece at any celebration or gathering and it tastes as good as it looks!

METHOD

To make the base, mix the digestive crumbs and sugar together, then pour over the melted butter and toss to coat. Press firmly into the bottom of a 23cm springform tin, making sure it's nice and compact. Put in the fridge for at least 30 minutes, until set.

Preheat the oven to 140°C.

To prepare the apples, melt the butter in a small saucepan over a medium heat. When the butter is foaming, add the apples, sugar and cinnamon. Cook gently for 6 to 8 minutes, until the apples are softened, then remove from the heat and set aside to cool.

Beat the cream cheese and sugar together for 3 to 4 minutes, until well combined, then add the eggs and cinnamon and beat again for 3 minutes more. Fold in half the apples, then spoon on top of the biscuit base and spread out into an even layer. Bake in the preheated oven for 40 minutes.

Meanwhile, to make the hazelnut crumble topping, put the flour, sugar and cinnamon in a bowl and mix to combine, then add the diced butter and use your fingertips to rub it in until it resembles coarse breadcrumbs. Stir in the hazelnuts.

After the initial 40 minutes, remove the cheesecake from the oven. Gently scatter the remaining apple on top, followed by the hazelnut crumble. Bake for a further 20 minutes, until it has set and is firm to the touch.

Allow to cool in the tin on a wire rack. When the cheesecake is completely cool, cover the top of the tin with foil and chill it in the fridge for 8 hours or overnight to allow it to firm up.

Run a knife around the edge before removing it from the tin and cutting into slices to serve.

For the base:
350g digestive biscuits, bashed into crumbs
50g caster sugar
150g butter, melted

For the apples:
25g butter
3 Granny Smith apples, peeled, cored and diced
25g caster sugar
1 tsp ground cinnamon

For the cheesecake mix:
400g cream cheese
150g caster sugar
3 eggs
1 tsp ground cinnamon

For the hazelnut crumble:
100g plain flour
75g Demerara sugar
½ tsp ground cinnamon
75g butter, chilled and diced
50g hazelnuts, roughly chopped

Our chefs let us in on a little secret...

CHEF'S TIP

This is best made a day ahead to allow the flavours to develop.

Raspberry Posset
with Lemon Polenta Biscuits

Serves 4

Originating from our Avoca Dunboyne kitchen, the crunch of the lemon polenta biscuits against the zingy raspberry posset is a winning combination that's perfect for a summer gathering. Fresh raspberries work best, but if they're out of season, frozen will do just fine.

METHOD

To make the posset, you first need to make a raspberry purée. Blitz the raspberries, icing sugar and a squeeze of lemon juice in a blender or food processor until smooth, then pass through a fine mesh sieve to strain out the seeds. Set aside.

Put the sugar and cream in a medium-sized saucepan on a low to medium heat and cook gently just until the sugar dissolves. Raise the heat to medium-high and bring to the boil, then continue to boil for 2 minutes, stirring constantly to make sure it doesn't catch on the bottom of the pan or quickly bubble up and over the sides of the saucepan.

Take the pan off the heat and stir in the raspberry purée. Allow to cool for 20 minutes before spooning the mixture into pretty serving glasses. Chill in the fridge for at least 2 hours, until set.

To make the biscuits, mix the flour and polenta together in a medium-sized bowl. In a separate bowl, beat the butter, sugar, vanilla and lemon zest together until pale and fluffy, then beat in the egg yolks and lemon juice. Add the dry ingredients and mix until it forms a dough, adding a tablespoon of water if needed to bring it together.

Roll the dough into a long sausage-like shape and wrap in cling film. Chill in the fridge for 1½ to 2 hours, until firm.

Continues ...

For the posset:
150g fresh raspberries
1 tsp icing sugar
a squeeze of lemon juice
110g caster sugar
500ml cream

For the lemon polenta biscuits:
180g self-raising flour
60g polenta
125g butter, at room
    temperature
125g caster sugar
1 tsp vanilla extract
zest of 1 lemon plus 1 tsp juice
2 egg yolks
icing sugar, for dusting

To decorate:
freeze-dried raspberries
    (optional)

METHOD CONTINUED

Preheat the oven to 170°C. Line a baking tray with non-stick baking paper.

Cut the roll of dough into biscuits 1cm thick and place on the lined baking tray, spaced a bit apart. Bake in the preheated oven for 10 to 12 minutes, until golden brown.

Allow to cool completely on the tray, then dust with icing sugar. Serve with the chilled raspberry posset decorated with freeze-dried raspberries.

Lemon Meringue Pie

Serves 12

Lemon meringue pie is a classic and we've made ours with the most deliciously tangy homemade lemon curd (luckily, you'll have some left over as you don't need the whole batch for the pie). Topped with fluffy meringue and baked in the oven for a crisp and golden finish, this dessert is a summertime crowd-pleaser.

METHOD

To make the lemon curd, put the lemon zest and juice, sugar and butter in a large heatproof non-reactive bowl. Sit the bowl over a saucepan of water and bring to a simmer, making sure the water doesn't touch the bottom of the bowl. Stir continuously until the butter has melted.

Whisk the eggs and egg yolks together in a separate bowl, then stir them into the lemon mixture. Whisk until all the ingredients are well combined and cook for 18 to 20 minutes, still over the pan of simmering water. Keep stirring until the curd is creamy and thick enough to coat the back of a spoon – it will start to thicken when the temperature gets close to 70°C on a candy thermometer. Remove the bowl from the heat and allow to cool, stirring occasionally. It will thicken even more as it cools. Set aside.

To make the pastry base, cream the butter and sugar together in the bowl of a stand mixer fitted with the paddle attachment for 6 to 8 minutes on a medium speed, scraping down the sides of the bowl every 1 or 2 minutes, until pale and fluffy. Beat in the eggs one at a time, making sure each one is fully incorporated before adding the next one.

Mix the flour and salt together in a separate bowl, then add it to the butter, sugar and egg mixture, beating just until the pastry comes together. Shape into a thick disc, wrap in cling film and refrigerate for at least 1 hour.

Preheat the oven to 170°C. Grease a 23cm loose-bottomed tart tin.

Continues ...

For the lemon curd:
zest and juice of 8 lemons
 (you need 400ml juice)
320g caster sugar
225g unsalted butter, diced
8 eggs
200g egg yolks (10 large eggs
 should give you 200g of
 yolks, leaving the whites for
 the meringue)

For the pastry base:
200g butter, softened, plus
 extra for greasing
70g caster sugar
3 eggs
350g plain flour
½ tsp fine sea salt

For the Italian meringue:
360g caster sugar
90ml water
6 egg whites, at room
 temperature
½ tsp cream of tartar

Our chefs let us in on a little secret...

CHEF'S TIP

Give yourself a head start and make the pastry and curd ahead of time.

METHOD CONTINUED

Roll the pastry between two sheets of cling film or using a chilled marble rolling pin until it's about 5mm thick. Press the pastry into the tin using your fingertips, making sure to leave 3cm or 4cm overhanging the tin. Push the pastry into the corners using a rolled-up ball of leftover pastry dusted with flour. Prick the bottom of the pastry all over with the tines of a fork. Line the pastry with a piece of non-stick baking paper, then cover with a layer of ceramic baking beans, dried beans or rice deep enough to completely fill the base.

Bake in the preheated oven for 15 minutes, then remove the paper and the beans or rice and cook for a further 5 minutes, until golden and firm. Allow to cool on a wire rack.

Increase the oven temperature to 200°C.

To make the Italian meringue, put the sugar and water in a saucepan over a medium heat. Rest a candy thermometer in the liquid. Start to slowly whisk the egg whites in a stand mixer until just starting to foam, then add the cream of tartar and whisk again for 2 minutes. While whisking, the sugar syrup needs to reach 121°C. Brush down the sides of the saucepan with a pastry brush and a little water to stop crystals forming.

When the desired temperature has been reached, slowly pour the sugar syrup into the egg whites while still whisking. Keep the stream of liquid to the side of the bowl, as this will stop it splashing and allows the syrup to cool slightly before it reaches the egg whites. Turn the whisk up to full speed and whisk until cooled to room temperature.

Fill the pastry base halfway with the lemon curd. Pipe or spread the meringue on top of the lemon curd and bake in the oven for 4 to 5 minutes, until the filling is set and the meringue is crisp and has turned a lovely golden colour. Alternatively, you could use a kitchen blowtorch to colour the meringue instead of baking the pie in the oven.

Allow to sit in the tin on a wire rack to cool for at least 1 hour before cutting into slices to serve.

TRAYBAKES & BISCUITS

Meeting for coffee and a sweet treat is probably the most
cherished Avoca ritual. We're famous for our traybakes, cookies
and biscuits, which are made to be shared. Try your hand at
some of our most-loved treats to recreate this ritual at home.
Box them up to share on a picnic, bring them as a gift to a
friend or eat warm from the oven at your table with a steaming
mug of tea or coffee.

A little bit of
nostalgia, a lot
of *tradition*.

Oat & Seed Bars

Makes 9 to 12

A delicious treat with a coffee or perfect as a breakfast on the go, these crunchy-yet-chewy bars are wonderfully simple to prepare. Once you've made this recipe a few times, play around with the ingredients to make it your own: swap the pecans for peanuts, or the dates for cranberries or sultanas.

METHOD

Preheat the oven to 140°C. Line a 20cm square tin with non-stick baking paper, making sure you leave some paper overhanging the sides.

Melt the butter and honey together in a saucepan.

Toss all the dry ingredients together in a large bowl, then add to the melted butter and honey, stirring until well combined.

Tip out into the lined tin and spread out evenly, then press down firmly – the mixture needs to be quite compact.

Bake in the preheated oven for 35 to 40 minutes, until golden brown and firm. Allow to cool slightly on a wire rack before using the paper to lift out of the tin. Cut into bars while still warm – you should get nine to 12 bars.

Allow to cool fully before storing in an airtight container. These will keep for up to five days.

100g butter
100g honey
180g porridge oats
100g light brown sugar
60g pitted dates
60g pecans, chopped
60g pumpkin seeds
60g dried apricots, chopped
30g ground almonds
30g sesame seeds
1 tsp ground cinnamon

Almond Squares

Makes 12

First made in Avoca Moll's Gap, these almond squares were such a hit that they were soon added to all our bakery counters. Divine!

METHOD

Preheat the oven to 180°C. Line a 23cm x 33cm Swiss roll tin with non-stick baking paper.

Put the flour, butter, sugar, egg yolks and vanilla in a food processor and blitz to combine. Tip out into the prepared tin, pressing firmly all along the base. Prick the pastry all over the base with a fork. Cover with a piece of non-stick baking paper and add enough ceramic baking beans or dried beans or rice to come halfway up the sides of the tin.

Blind bake in the preheated oven for 10 minutes, then remove the beans and paper and bake for another 10 minutes, until golden.

Meanwhile, to make the topping, put the flaked almonds, butter, brown sugar and honey in the bowl of a stand mixer with the paddle attachment fitted. Mix on a medium speed for 5 minutes, until it has turned a pale straw colour, then add the cream and mix on a low speed for 1 minute more.

Spread the mix evenly over the cooked pastry base with a small palette knife. It should be about 1.5cm to 2cm thick.

Bake in the oven for about 10 minutes, just until the topping turns a light golden brown. Remove from the oven and scatter over more flaked almonds to decorate, then return to the oven and bake for another 5 minutes.

Allow to cool completely on a wire rack, then cut into squares. These will keep in an airtight container for up to five days.

For the pastry base:
340g plain flour
220g butter, diced
60g caster sugar
2 egg yolks
1 tsp vanilla essence

For the topping:
250g flaked almonds, plus extra to decorate
130g butter, at room temperature
70g light brown sugar
70ml honey
3 tbsp fresh cream

Cookie Sandwiches
with Hazelnut Filling

Makes 6

A gleefully decadent recipe for those times when a traditional cookie just won't do!

METHOD

To make the cookies, beat the butter and sugar together until pale and creamy, then beat in the egg yolk and vanilla.

Mix the flour and baking soda together, then add to the butter and sugar. Mix together with a spatula or wooden spoon until combined, then stir in the chocolate chips.

Spread a large piece of cling film on the countertop. Tip the dough out onto the cling film and roll into a 5cm-thick sausage shape. Wrap tightly and refrigerate for 45 minutes to 1 hour, until set firm.

Preheat the oven to 170°C. Line two baking trays with non-stick baking paper.

Cut the log of dough into discs 1cm thick and place on the lined baking trays, leaving a 5cm gap in between as they will expand and flatten as they cook. Bake in the preheated oven for 10 to 12 minutes, until golden. Transfer to a wire rack and allow to cool completely on the trays.

Meanwhile, to make the filling, whip the cream until soft peaks form.

In a separate bowl, mix together the mascarpone, hazelnut butter and icing sugar with an electric hand mixer, then fold in the whipped cream.

To assemble, take 2 heaped tablespoons of the filling and place it on one cookie, flat side facing up, and spread it out but not all the way to the edges. Scatter over 1 teaspoon of the crushed hazelnuts, then sandwich together with another cookie.

225g butter, at room
 temperature
225g caster sugar
1 large egg yolk
1 tsp vanilla extract
250g plain flour
½ tsp baking soda
250g chocolate chips

For the filling:
100ml cream
250g mascarpone cheese
100g hazelnut butter
120g icing sugar
a big handful of toasted
 hazelnuts, crushed

Bakewell Squares
with a Cherry on Top

Makes 9 to 12

A little bit retro and a whole lot delicious, a Bakewell tart is another Avoca classic and this fail-safe recipe turns out perfect Bakewells every time. The icing is optional, so you can choose how best to enjoy.

METHOD

To make the pastry base, put the flour, butter, sugar, egg yolks and vanilla in a food processor and pulse just until it forms a dough. Roll into a disc, cover with cling film and chill in the fridge for at least 1 hour.

Preheat the oven to 170°C.

Roll out the dough between two large sheets of cling film (or use a chilled marble rolling pin if you have one) so that it fits the base and sides of a 23cm x 33cm Swiss roll tin.

Warm and loosen the jam slightly first in a small saucepan or in the microwave, then spread it evenly over the pastry base.

To make the frangipane layer, put the butter and sugar in a large bowl and beat until smooth and creamy (or use a stand mixer fitted with the paddle attachment). Beat in the eggs one at a time, adding 1 tablespoon of ground almonds after each egg.

Once all the eggs have been incorporated, add the rest of the ground almonds along with the flour and almond extract and mix well. Spoon the mixture over the jam, spreading it out into an even layer.

Bake in the preheated oven for 35 to 40 minutes, until golden and firm. Transfer to a wire rack and leave to cool completely in the tin.

Continues ...

For the pastry base:
340g plain flour
220g butter, diced
60g caster sugar
2 egg yolks
1 tsp vanilla essence

For the jam layer:
400g strawberry jam

For the frangipane layer:
200g butter, at room temperature
200g caster sugar
4 eggs
100g ground almonds
100g self-raising flour
1 tsp almond extract

For the icing (optional):
300g icing sugar, sifted
3 tbsp water

To decorate:
6 glacé cherries, halved
20g flaked almonds, toasted

Our chefs let us in on a little secret

CHEF'S TIP

Use a seedless strawberry preserve instead of jam for a smoother texture.

METHOD CONTINUED

To make the icing (if using), whisk together the icing sugar and water to make a fairly thick icing. When the tart is cold, spoon the icing on top, spreading it out evenly. Score the Bakewell where you're going to cut it into squares and place a cherry, cut side down, in the middle of each square, then scatter over the toasted flaked almonds.

Cut into squares, making sure each square has a cherry on top. These will keep in an airtight container for up to five days.

Chocolate Brownies
with Toasted Pecans & Caramel Sauce

Makes 9 to 12

These brownies are pure decadence. Never known to shy away from a little indulgence, we've taken the classic chocolate brownie up a notch with the addition of toasted pecans and a rich caramel sauce.

METHOD

Preheat the oven to 180°C.

Scatter the pecans over a small baking tray and roast in the preheated oven for 10 minutes, until nicely toasted. Allow to cool, then roughly chop.

When the pecans come out of the oven, reduce the temperature to 160°C and line a 20cm square brownie tin with non-stick baking paper.

To make the brownies, mix together the sugar, cocoa powder and flour in a large bowl.

Put the chocolate and butter in a heatproof bowl set over a pan of simmering water, making sure the water doesn't touch the bottom of the bowl. Once they have melted together, add the beaten eggs and half the pecans. Using a spatula, scrape into the dry ingredients and mix in gently until just combined.

Pour the batter into the lined tin and bake in the preheated oven. Start checking them after 15 minutes, but they may need up to 30 minutes – you want them to be barely set with a little jiggle. This ensures you'll get that slightly chewy texture that you want in a brownie.

Set on a wire rack and allow to cool in the tin for at least 30 minutes.

Continues ...

100g pecans
275g caster sugar
80g cocoa powder
50g self-raising flour
160g chocolate (at least 55% cocoa content), chopped
125g butter, diced
4 eggs, beaten until doubled in size

For the caramel sauce:
225g caster sugar
4 tbsp water
45g butter, diced
130ml cream

To serve:
vanilla ice cream

METHOD CONTINUED

While the brownies are cooling, make the caramel. Spread the caster sugar around the base of a saucepan and add the water. Cook on a medium heat for 6 to 8 minutes, swirling the pan now and then, until the sugar has dissolved and turned a golden caramel colour. Do not stir the sugar at this stage and do not allow it to cook beyond a medium-brown colour – if it turns dark brown, it means you have gone too far because it will darken even further as it cools, so you will have to start all over again. Once you are happy with the colour, add the butter and cream together and stir with a wooden spoon. Allow the caramel sauce to cool in the pan before transferring to a pouring jug.

Cut the cooled brownies into nine to 12 equal pieces and remove from the tin. Serve with a scoop of vanilla ice cream, pour over the caramel sauce and scatter over the remaining toasted pecans.

White Rocky Road

with Macadamia Nuts & Raspberries

Makes 16

Always a hit at birthday parties, this rocky road is also the
perfect Christmas treat thanks to its festive colour scheme.

METHOD

Line a 20cm square brownie tin with non-stick baking
paper.

Toast the macadamia nuts in a hot dry frying pan over a
medium heat for 3 to 4 minutes, until they begin to turn
golden brown. Tip out onto a plate and allow to cool.

Put the white chocolate, butter and golden syrup in a
large heatproof bowl set over a pan of simmering water,
making sure the water doesn't touch the bottom of the
bowl. Once the chocolate and butter have melted, stir in
the orange zest.

Remove the bowl from the pan. Working fast, stir in
the toasted macadamia nuts along with the digestives,
cherries, apricots and cranberries – the mixture will start
to set quite quickly. Scrape into the lined tin, then scatter
over the freeze-dried raspberries. Refrigerate for at least 2
hours but preferably overnight, until set firm.

Allow to sit at room temperature for 20 minutes before
cutting into small squares with a hot knife. Simply dip a
sharp knife into a measuring jug of just-boiled water from
the kettle, then wipe it dry and use immediately.

70g macadamia nuts
600g white chocolate, chopped
70g butter, diced
2 tbsp golden syrup
zest of 1 orange
150g digestive biscuits, broken
    into bite-sized pieces
70g glacé cherries
15g dried apricots, chopped
15g dried cranberries
15g freeze-dried raspberries

Macadamia & White Chocolate Cookies

Makes approx. 20

What began as simple macadamia nut cookies evolved into these truly decadent double chocolate wonders with their two-tone drizzle.

METHOD

Preheat the oven to 160°C. Line two baking trays with non-stick baking paper. Sift the flour and baking powder into a large bowl and set aside.

Put both sugars and the melted butter, egg, egg yolk and vanilla in a separate bowl and beat together until creamy. Add the flour mixture and stir together until just combined, then stir in the white chocolate and macadamia nuts. Taking approx. 40g of dough at a time, roll it into a ball and place on the lined trays, leaving 3cm or 4cm between each cookie.

Bake in the preheated oven for 12 to 15 minutes, until light golden. If you cook them for only 12 minutes and slightly underbake them, you'll get a softer, chewier cookie. If you prefer your cookies to have more crunch, bake for the full 15 minutes. Allow to cool on the tray for 10 minutes, then transfer to a wire rack.

When the cookies have cooled, melt the dark chocolate by putting it in a microwave-safe bowl and microwaving in 30-second increments just until it has melted. This should take 2 to 2½ minutes.

Repeat to melt the white chocolate in a separate bowl but microwave it for only 15 seconds at a time, otherwise the white chocolate can overcook and turn crumbly.

Dip a fork into the melted dark chocolate and drizzle it over the cookies from left to right. Scatter over the extra chopped macadamia nuts, then repeat with the melted white chocolate.

250g plain flour
1 tsp baking powder
210g light brown sugar
110g caster sugar
170g butter, melted
1 egg
1 egg yolk
1 tsp vanilla extract
200g white chocolate,
    roughly chopped
100g macadamia nuts,
    roughly chopped

For the topping:
125g dark chocolate,
    chopped
125g white chocolate,
    chopped
50g macadamia nuts,
    chopped

We think you'll love this...

EXTRA EXTRA

Double the batch and keep half wrapped up in the freezer for home-baked cookies hot from the oven on demand!

Anzac Biscuits

Makes 16 to 18

Inspired by the classic biscuit from Australia and New Zealand, these buttery, coconutty treats can be rolled in non-stick baking paper and frozen that so you can bake a fresh batch whenever your heart desires.

METHOD

Preheat the oven to 160°C. Line two baking trays with non-stick baking paper.

Gently melt the butter and golden syrup together in a small saucepan over a medium heat. Stir in the baking soda until it foams up, then stir in the water.

Mix the flour, sugar, oats and coconut together in a large bowl, then pour in the melted butter mixture and stir to combine.

Take tablespoons of the dough (about 30g) and with damp hands, roll them into balls. Place on the lined baking trays spaced 2.5cm apart. Bake in the preheated oven for 10 minutes, until golden.

Remove from the oven and allow to sit on the trays for 10 minutes to firm up, then transfer to a wire rack to cool completely.

100g butter, melted
75g golden syrup
1 tsp baking soda
2 tbsp water
90g plain flour
90g caster sugar
85g porridge oats
85g desiccated coconut

THANK YOU!

The first most heartfelt thank you simply has to go to the fabulous chefs from our restaurants, cafés, bakeries and central kitchen – a creative and dedicated bunch of passionate foodies, who approached this cookbook with huge generosity and enthusiasm. We're so grateful to them for sharing their most-loved, tried and tested recipes, whether passed down from great-grannies, trusted family favourites or accidentally delicious concoctions rustled up at home. The most difficult job was narrowing the selection down to fit within the page limit! Quite simply, this cookbook wouldn't have happened without our chefs, and we're beyond grateful for your hard work and talent.

Thank you to Ivor and Justin, our trusted double act for recipe-testing – and testing again, and again! – until each and every recipe was just right. We are so grateful to you, Ivor, for taking on the mammoth task of cherry-picking from and collating the wonderful recipes submitted. Adding a side of guacamole here, a slight modification to cooking time there, you were always happy to roll with it, not resting until each dish was perfect for the home cook. It was no mean feat – after all, how do you turn 'a dollop' into a measurement?!

The beautiful food photography in these pages is thanks to our incredibly talented photographer and friend, Trevor Hart. A perfect match for our ridiculous levels of perfectionism, we are so thankful for all of your artistic input, talent and hard work on this project, as well as your readiness to shoot some of the dishes 'just one more time' until we were all above and beyond happy with each image.

We absolutely would not have made it to the end of this project without our prop stylist Eleanor Harpur, whose organisation, creativity and wicked sense of humour are simply second to none. Thank you for sharing your somehow bottomless range of treasures and wares that helped us create our vision for *Avoca at Home* so beautifully.

Huge thanks to our wonderful food stylist, Johan Van der Mewe, and assistant food stylist Conaill O'Dwyer for their endless hours of shopping, chopping, prepping, cooking and styling – and for feeding us every lunch time in the studio. Endlessly cool, calm and collected in the kitchen, it was such a pleasure working, and laughing, with you both.

To the fabulous editorial photographer, Doreen Kilfeather – thank you for bringing our vision to life. Your energy and creativity are inspiring and infectious, and you always manage to get absolute magic from the kids (and animals – especially Fluffy the dog!) on our shoots. To our wonderful stylist, Ruth Kennedy Forsyth, thank you for always bringing your fabulously effortless touch to everything you do, and doing it all with a smile on your face. Thank you to our wonderful model Faye – we've loved working with you on every shoot we have done together over the years. And, of course, we also have to give a special mention to our beautiful young models Bonnie, Dolly, Nancy, Ellie and Cloud. How do you all never get tired?

Shane, Frank and Derek, we're so grateful for your incredible support and encouragement with this project. Thank you to Maoliosa, the driving force behind our Avoca team who made this cookbook happen. You're a tour de force and we love how you add your characteristic sparkle and shine to everything you do.

Thank you to our incredible creative team. Your tireless work on this book, long days, sleepless nights and endless pursuit of perfection, it was definitely worth it! Gill, you (somehow) manage to think of everything and have been the guiding light for all of us. Thank you for leading the way in all things creative for this cookbook, as well as for your never-failing sense of humour, endless supply of family heirlooms, warmth and kindness. Alex, thank you for your incredible attention to detail, beautiful typography, perfect illustrations, endless laughs and for crossing the Irish sea at a moment's notice whenever we needed you by our sides. Caroline, for your beautiful words, your incredible patience and good humour at yet another table read. You have brought this book to life for us all.

Thanks to Ciara for calmly being there to walk through this with us and answering the endless 'what do you think' questions, and Loren thank you for those beautiful templates you managed to do when the rest of us had run out of steam. And thank you to April – everyone's best friend at the office, we don't know what we'd do without you.

Thank you, too, to the wider creative and marketing teams for all of your input, reading and re-reading, and at-home recipe testing with your friends and families! It takes a village to write a cookbook and we couldn't have done it without you all.

A special thank you is also in order for Michael, Patricia and Issy at Penguin Sandycove. Thank you for keeping our unruly team in check and on deadline. Even though we know we almost broke your hearts, it was a huge comfort going through this whole project with your guidance and expertise. We liked the 'cut of your jib' since our very first virtual Teams call!

Last but definitely not least – thank you to our wonderful, loyal customers for celebrating with us and including Avoca in your homes and family traditions over the years. All of the coffee and cake meet-ups, birthday celebrations, family dinners, anniversaries and more that we've been lucky enough to play a little part of – we are honoured, and so grateful.

INDEX

C

SANDYCOVE

UK | USA | Canada | Ireland | Australia
India | New Zealand | South Africa

Sandycove is part of the Penguin Random House group of companies
whose addresses can be found at global.penguinrandomhouse.com.

First published 2022
001

Creative director: Gill Mooney
Design and illustrations: Alex Whyte
Copywriter: Caroline Cruikshank
Food photography: Trevor Hart
Food stylist: Johan Van der Mewe
Assistant food stylist: Conaill O'Dwyer
Prop stylist: Eleanor Harpur
Editorial photography: Doreen Kilfeather
Editorial stylist: Ruth Kennedy Forsyth

Colour reproduction by AltaImage, London
Printed and bound in Italy by Printer Trento

The authorized representative in the EEA is Penguin Random House Ireland, Morrison Chambers,
32 Nassau Street, Dublin D02 YH68

A CIP catalogue record for this book is available from the British Library

ISBN: 978–1–844–88590–9